EDUCATING CHARACTER THROUGH STORIES

**DAVID CARR
AND TOM HARRISON**

imprint-academic.com

Published in the UK by
Imprint Academic, PO Box 200, Exeter EX5 5YX, UK

Distributed in the USA by
Ingram Book Company,
One Ingram Blvd., La Vergne, TN 37086, USA

ISBN 9781845407803

A CIP catalogue record for this book is available from the
British Library and US Library of Congress

The index for this volume was produced by
Indexing Specialists (UK) Ltd.

Contents

The Knightly
Virtues

Humility · Honesty · Gratitude · Self-Discipline · Love · Justice · Courage · Service

Knightly Virtues

These *vitues* are the qualities that make us *special*

Professor James Arthur

Foreword

The formation of character could be said to be the aim that all general education has historically set out to achieve. It is an aim that has often not been explicitly stated, instead it has simply been assumed. Today there is a growing debate about the merits of character education and there is a growing body of evidence, based on sound theory, demonstrating that character education is not only a worthwhile educational pursuit in its own right, but that it can and should be part of the solution to many of the challenges facing society today. Character education is being taken increasingly seriously by policy makers, practitioners, employers, the voluntary sector as well as many others. However, what is missing, in Britain at least, is high quality character education teaching materials that have been rigorously evaluated before being implemented in schools.

The Knightly Virtues programme, run by the Jubilee Centre for Character and Virtues at the University of Birmingham, offers a new teaching resource to schools. It is an inspirational teaching programme that is easy for teachers to integrate into the curriculum and it is having a significant impact on the young people who experience it. It has also been immensely popular with primary schools across Britain with hundreds signing up over the last few years to deliver the programme.

This book, *Educating Character Through Stories*, explores the theory behind the Knightly Virtues programme, as well as its practical applications.

It provides not only a theoretical and conceptual basis, but also offers empirical support, for the educational use of stories. This solid evidence provides a compelling case for the use of stories as the basis for the exploration and cultivation of the character strengths and virtues. As such, the book raises many questions, but also offers some answers to the pressing moral questions of today—not least, what kind of person do we want our children to grow up to be.

Professor James Arthur
Director of the Jubilee Centre for Character and Virtues
Head of the School of Education, University of Birmingham

Introduction

This book has three main aims. The first is to defend and further illuminate a fairly time-honoured conviction that the education of children and young people should extend beyond the learning of academic subjects and/or useful skills to comprehend the development of moral and social values, and—perhaps even more than this—to the cultivation of personal moral character. In this regard, something will need to be said about what is here meant—as well as not meant—by the term 'character'. To this end, the present work will draw on some fairly 'reader-friendly' ideas from the ancient philosopher Aristotle whose pioneering work on moral or virtuous character has been subject to widespread contemporary academic, professional and educational revival. On the back of this, however, we will attempt some justification of character education as a legitimate aim of school or other education, with especial reference to the reasons why character education—and/or the widespread failure or neglect of latter schooling to give proper attention to character education—has become a matter of global concern to educational theorists, politicians and policy makers, teachers, parents and the general public. From this viewpoint, as we shall see, it seems hard to deny that there has been an enormous popular groundswell in favour of character education.

The second, rather more central, aim of the work—for which the more general observations on character and character education set the stage—is to drive home the point that, among the many possible educational routes to the development or education of moral character, the use of stories from past and present day imaginative literature is perhaps the most promising and potent. In making this claim, the authors once again draw on the philosophical authority of Aristotle—as well as upon some reworking of Aristotle's ideas by the more recent moral and social theorist Alasdair MacIntyre—to the effect that stories and narratives of cultural or literary inheritance have a power to illuminate moral and other aspects of human motivation, feeling and agency in a way that other (say natural or social scientific) sources of knowledge and insight are not well (if at all) placed to provide. To be sure, MacIntyre goes so far as to say that it is only possible for us to see ourselves as human persons or agents operating in a space of moral or other goals, purposes and choices as something like characters in a story: that, in short, narratives provide something like the logical form or contours of human self-understanding. Moreover, from the perspective of character education, it hardly needs saying that much imaginative literature—from the very dawn of human storytelling—has been precisely concerned to explore the lighter and darker, heroic and demonic, aspects of human character in often painful detail.

However, the main point of the fairly protracted exploration of the moral educational value and potential of stories of this work is to try to help teachers, parents and others involved in the moral education and character formation of children and young people to understand better how stories might be utilized to promote such goals. That said, the present work is not a 'how to do it' book of the sort that offers prescribed lesson plans for the achievement of set learning objectives in the manner of some latter day aids to professional practice. Simply, moral and character development through stories is not the sort of thing that readily lends itself to such treatment. On the contrary, cultural or literary stories of enduring moral worth are invariably narratives of a human significance, complexity and ambivalence that cannot be understood or addressed without serious, authentic and educated immersion in or engagement with them.

Since there are no quick or easy 'tips' for understanding and communicating the moral significance of such stories, what is therefore required is precisely an appropriately educated sensibility and sensitivity to such fare on the part of those who would teach them to others. It is some sense of this that the key chapters on understanding the potential of literature for character education — by which, of course, we generally mean the education of *moral* character — seek to provide in this work. Here, to be sure, we are duly appreciative of the point that not all school teachers are teachers of literature. We are well aware that contemporary schooling in modern societies requires the educational promotion of advanced and specialist — often highly technical — knowledge in a wide range of fields that teachers often have their work cut out to keep up with. At the same time, we take the view that the first requirement for being any sort of teacher is to be an educated person oneself — one who thereby professes at least some serious interest in those larger moral and other questions of human life and association that have nowhere been better treated than in the great imaginative art and literature of cultural inheritance. From this viewpoint, we believe that it behoves all those who would seriously claim to be preparing children for a life of moral, spiritual and cultural fullness — rather than merely teaching them this or that disconnected skill — to have some educated acquaintance with the broader concerns of the human condition about which the greatest of past and present minds have sought to enlighten us.

Here, by the way, we are well aware of previous fine work on the use of literature for moral character education — notably Karen Bohlin's excellent book on teaching character through literature (Bohlin 2005) — that we would regard as welcome fellow travellers along the present road. However, we also hope that the present contribution, particularly in the context of the project shortly to be described, brings something of added value to such previous work. Indeed, this brings us fairly neatly to the third key aim of this work, which is to say something of (we hope) practical value to others about a project lately pursued by the Jubilee Centre for the Study of Character and Virtues based at the University of Birmingham. This project had its origins in an attempt to respond positively to the prospect of John Templeton Foundation funding for some school-based moral educational work or programme that might explore ideals of nobility, honour and service (*noblesse oblige*) often or generally (since, of course, one can easily think of past and present incumbents of this title who have been rather far from upholding such ideals) associated with British and wider European traditions and institutions of knighthood and other nobility. In fact, this prospect was greeted with particular enthusiasm by one present author as sitting perfectly with work on the value of literature and other creative and imaginative art for moral character education in which he has already been engaged for some decades. It was also fairly apparent from the most casual survey of contemporary literature, television and cinema that one theme of timeless attraction and fascination for children and young people—of well-nigh all classes, cultures and genders—is that of the heroic deeds and exploits of medieval knights in shining armour, perhaps exemplified above all in the perennially reworked British legend or myth of King Arthur and his Knights of the Round Table. It is not just that such stories clearly have enduring appeal for young people, but— more importantly—that once one reaches behind the surface derring-do or martial arts knock-about of such stories to the deeper themes explored by such authors as Malory and Tennyson, it is abundantly clear that they offer scope for exploration of human association and moral or virtuous character of peerless insight. Indeed, we have tried to make this particularly clear in (for example) our exploration in Chapter 4 of the profound lessons to be learned about the nature of true love and virtue from Malory's insightful treatment of the Lancelot and Guinevere narrative.

At all events, what has come to be called — with great affection though, as we shall see, no longer complete accuracy — the 'Knightly Virtues' project, has now been running in British schools for over two years to almost universal acclaim. There can be little doubt that teachers in schools, school pupils and their parents have taken to the project like proverbial ducks to water and that the use of past stories from great literature has now been shown to make a significant positive contribution to the understanding of children and young people of the language of moral virtue and character — and also of their appreciation of the complexity of moral life and association — if not to the actual practical improvement of conduct (which many teachers and parents claim it has also had). That said, it is not merely the purpose of the last two chapters of this work for the architects and school-based developers of the Knightly Virtues programme to congratulate themselves on a job well done, but also to offer some insight into the logistical challenges — however eventually surmountable — of fitting a fairly pioneering project of this kind into the officially prescribed curricula of state schooling, to provide some overview of the teaching resources and strategies developed to support the programme, to give some flavour of the responses of pupils, teachers and parents to the project and to suggest directions for further or future development of work to date.

Towards all these ends, the present work develops through seven chapters. Following this introduction, Chapter 1 attempts to set the stage by outlining — with much reference to recent British and other educational history — the pressing present-day case for more explicit attention to moral and character education than has hitherto been apparent in contemporary state schooling. While this chapter attempts to offer some sympathetic reasons for such apparent neglect of broader attention to moral character in latter day schooling — acknowledging (for example) recent

unease about the school teaching of moral values – it argues
that clearer philosophical thinking may enable us to see that
such unease is largely misplaced and that there is no reason
to think that appropriate moral character education cannot
or should not be a going contemporary educational concern.
That said, Chapter 2 turns to the more direct concern of this
work with the moral educational uses of story and narrative,
arguing – against time-honoured scepticism reaching back at
least to Plato – that imaginative literature can and should be
regarded as an important if not indeed indispensable source
of insights into the human moral condition in general and
into moral character more particularly. Following Aristotle,
this chapter argues that imaginative literature has a
particular contribution to make to emotional education and
to the cultivation of morally sound feeling and affect.
Chapter 3 attempts to drive this point further home with
fairly extensive exploration of respects in which different
literary genres have variously contributed to our understanding of moral life and character. Here, it is argued that
while some great cultural and literary works seem to have
focused on large philosophical questions about the human
moral and spiritual condition and others have focused in
more detail on the complexities of human character, much
past literature – such as the great dramas of Euripides or
Shakespeare – have addressed both kinds of issue in
interesting interplay.

Closer to the Knightly Virtues project, however, Chapter
4 concentrates more directly on the historically problematic
and morally ambivalent virtues of 'knighthood' of medieval
chivalry as exemplified or celebrated in the stories of King
Arthur and his Knights of the Round Table in the works of
Sir Thomas Malory, Alfred Lord Tennyson and others.
Following from this, attention is turned in Chapter 5 to the
four key stories of the Knightly Virtues project, wherein –
after fairly full descriptions or accounts of each of these
stories – some exploration of their educational significance is
offered by way of possible guidance for their classroom

teaching. In Chapter 6, as already indicated, the authors offer some account of the teaching resources, materials and strategies used to support the Knightly Virtues programme in schools as well as of the curricular and other challenges encountered in its practical implementation. Finally, in the light of contemporary concerns about parent-school partnership and related issues, Chapter 7 provides some account of pupil, teacher and parent reactions to the project in the context of larger critical evaluation of where the Knightly Virtues might go from here.

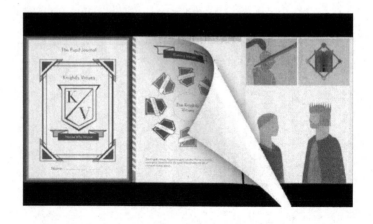

Chapter One

The Case for Character Education

Character as a Key Educational Concern

If asked what schools are for, the answer that most people would be likely to give is that they are for the *education* of children and young people. However, given the public, professional and philosophical debates that have raged from ancient times to the present over the aims and purposes of education, it might well be complained that this observation gets us little further. Still, conceding that schools do and should have educational aims and purposes — which, since this has been denied by some modern radical educationalists, is not entirely beyond dispute — we might here distinguish between *narrower* and *broader* conceptions of the aims of schooling. On a narrower view, the education of schooling is primarily a matter of formal provision of basic skills of literacy and numeracy, traditional academic subject learning — primarily for the certification required for entry into higher education or other post-school occupations — and/or some of the vocational skills required for adult post-school work. In short, on this view, schooling is largely for the development or acquisition of instrumentally (perhaps economically) *useful* knowledge and skills, and good teaching is the effective and efficient promotion or transmission of such capacities and abilities.

On a broader or more expansive view, however, school or other education cannot or should not be reduced to such narrow academic or vocational learning and ought precisely to embrace wider personal development of the kind the ancients identified with moral or 'virtuous' character. Or, to put this as so put by Socrates in Plato's great dialogue *Gorgias* (Plato 1961), the basic educational question is not that of what might usefully be learned to succeed or get ahead in life — especially if this is understood only in terms of material prosperity — but that of what may reasonably be *considered to be* a good life, and of how one might become the sort of person capable of living such a life. Another way of putting this point might be to say that education should be concerned with the discernment and promotion of (moral and other) ends and purposes that are valuable not merely as *means* to other ends, but *in and of themselves*. In this light, to show that the learning of (for example) Shakespeare's *Romeo and Juliet* or the causes of the First World War is of real *educational* value, one would need to show that it involves more than just memorization of so many facts for examination or other external purposes — which might also be conveniently forgotten once the instrumental uses are no longer in view: precisely, one would need to show that it makes some *intrinsically* worthwhile contribution to learners' knowledge and understanding of themselves, their world and their relations with others. On this view, any education of much significance or substance could not be — at least exclusively — a mere (contingent) means to some further end, and should be an initiation into enquiries, activities or pursuits that are at least potentially *constitutive* of a meaningful life.

That said, while some capacity to engage in activities as ends rather than means may be a *necessary* mark of education so conceived, it is clearly not *sufficient*. For there would seem to be many activities in which people might so engage — such as reading horror comics, watching junk TV or playing Russian roulette — that are not obviously of much educational or other positive human value. In this light, any worthwhile educational activity should also conduce to some demonstrable human worth or benefit. In short, we need to be able to make some (rational) case that it contributes to the wellbeing or flourishing of those engaged in it. For Socrates, this meant that any such activity would have to be consistent with what is objectively *true* and *good*. Precisely, the Socratic case against the ancient Greek sophists — in Plato's *Gorgias* and elsewhere — rested on the point that insofar as their teachings were at odds with truth and justice, they could not be genuinely educational. Notably, the art of rhetoric that Gorgias and other sophists considered the most useful of human skills — on account of its effectiveness in persuading others to our cause or point of view — could not be educational if such persuasion served immorally manipulative, dishonest or unjust ends. No doubt Hitler was a master of rhetoric; but his powers of persuasion served no human good.

Plato's *Gorgias* is of no less interest to students of education and teaching today than it was then — precisely because it sets out so clearly what may go wrong if educational theorizing overplays the significance of shallow notions of personal ambition or economic growth. Still, while it seems nowadays widely felt — and is no less often said — that this is the way in which much contemporary schooling has gone, there is also some danger of pessimistic overstatement or exaggeration of latter day educational developments. For, despite its undoubted shortcomings, most contemporary institutionalized schooling in developed countries clearly benefits the young in ways that their parents — or at least not too remote ancestors — could barely have imagined. While there may still be injustices and inequalities, much modern state education has also been driven by philanthropic and egalitarian motives to try to level a field of social and economic opportunity in what is in many places — for historical reasons — often extremely uneven for many people. Moreover, those who enter the teaching profession are also invariably driven by philanthropic and egalitarian goals of service to others, they work extremely long and hard to achieve such goals and they more often than not do a highly

commendable job. So what then is the basic worry of those —
such as the present authors — who seem to see contemporary
schooling as somehow falling short of the broader Socratic
educational ideal lately noticed?

There has certainly been a conspicuous shift in conceptions of the role and purposes of school education in
Britain from the middle of the last century to the present
day. In fact, the present lines are written just seventy years
on from the British 1944 Education Act that explicitly sought
to afford unprecedented state educational opportunities to a
far wider secondary school population than had previously
been catered for. While there will be those who are quick to
point out that the 1944 Education Act actually engendered a
very unequal and segregated — precisely tri-partite and
hierarchical — state system of schooling, this was soon to be
overtaken in the nineteen sixties by the more egalitarian
reforms of comprehensive education. However, what may
now seem a striking difference between the 1944 Act and
many later educational reforms was its fairly traditional
British emphasis on the importance of the broader moral and
religious dimensions of school education. In this regard,
indeed, it is often pointed out that the only school activity
actually mandated by the Act was 'a daily act of (by implication Christian) worship'. While any such educational
requirement is clearly not, from a variety of social, moral and
other perspectives, unproblematic, it did register a sense —
however conscious or sincere — of the importance of promoting *some* set or system of moral beliefs, virtues and practices to British youth and potential citizens. From the perspective of the Act, Britain was a Christian country and it
was important to uphold and preserve — at both national
and personal levels — the values and virtues of a Christian
way of life. And daily worship was — *rightly or wrongly* —
considered conducive to this.

To be sure, all of this was and is highly problematic. The
1944 Act clearly reflected the traditional British association of
church and state — including state education — apparently

unmindful of the reasons why so many other western countries had precisely sought to separate these. Moreover, the problems of educationally maintaining such religious baggage were soon to become clear with the unprecedented increase of migration to Britain from former British colonies that occurred from the nineteen fifties onwards. Simply, the daily act of (Christian) worship could no longer make much sense in many British schools now populated mainly if not exclusively by Muslims, Hindus or other non-Christians. Still, the problem as perceived was clearly a much larger one. If education is significantly implicated in the trans-mission and acquisition of values and virtues, and—as the 1944 Act seems to have assumed—such virtues and values are grounded in or authorized by larger religious concep-tions of human flourishing, how might we promote *common* values and virtues in circumstances of cultural pluralism in which different faiths (or other ideological sources of value) evidently conflict at practical and moral as well as theo-logical and doctrinal levels?

The Educational Problem with Values and Virtues

The problem of how to transmit or teach moral values to the young—especially in contexts of public schooling—loomed large in the emerging 'analytical' revolution of philosophy of education perhaps most notably pioneered in post-WWII years by Israel Scheffler (1983) in the US and R.S. Peters (1966) in the UK. Assuming that moral values are rationally or otherwise grounded in larger religious or other visions of human flourishing of the kind that John Rawls (1999) famously dubbed 'comprehensive theories of the good', it was widely felt that no moral values could be promoted without risk of indoctrination. On this view, to teach that abortion is morally wrong or capital punishment is right would be to promote some partisan viewpoint of no 'objective' rational justification beyond this or that religious, political or other ideological authority or agenda. Hence, much late twentieth century discussion of the teaching of moral and other values—probably much influenced by the psychology of so-called 'values clarification' (see, for example, Simon *et al.* 1972)—focused on the possibility of the 'neutral teacher' (on this, see classic essays by Mary Warnock and John Wilson in Section II of Taylor 1975) who might stimulate or facilitate discussion of controversial issues without ever appearing to 'take sides'. It was understandable in the circumstances that professionally conscientious and sincere teachers of history, social studies and other subjects felt nervous about expressing their own personal opinions on any morally implicated issues of the day.

However, another major post-war response to this issue was to reject wholesale any idea that moral values would have to be grounded in or authorized by any religious or other 'ideological' perspective or worldview (Hirst 1974). In opposition to the perceived moral relativism of values clarification, and influenced by Jean Piaget's theory of cognitive development, as well as by the liberal accounts of justice of John Rawls and others, the Harvard psychologist Lawrence Kohlberg (1984) pioneered a stage theory of moral development and education firmly committed to neo-Kantian faith in the possibility of a moral reason or rationality entirely free of any compromising religious or other ideological baggage. On Kohlberg's view—which had distinct neo-Kantian parallels in accounts developed in Britain and elsewhere by the likes of R.S. Peters (1981) and the Oxford educational philosopher John Wilson (1990)—it was not just educationally desirable but imperative to teach people to deliberate to rationally 'objective' or 'disinterested' conclusions on the most vexed of moral issues and controversies. To be sure, individuals might be drawn to somewhat different moral conclusions on the basis of such reason, but they would be led to these by way of authentic or independent reflection rather than blind obedience to religious, political or other dogma or authority.

Still, in his haste to throw out the moral bathwater of blind adherence to controversial religious or other ideological doctrines or authorities, Kohlberg also arguably threw out the baby of moral character in rejecting what he scathingly called the 'bag of virtues' view of moral education (Kohlberg 1984). For Kohlberg, there seem to have been two main objections to traditional attempts to inculcate moral dispositions or habits of good—honest, fair, brave, self-controlled, compassionate and so on—conduct. The first was clearly ethical or *normative*: such attempts invariably involved obedience of the young to various sorts of authority—and it could be seen from very recent history what horrors conformity to nationalist, communist or religious fundamentalist authority could produce. The second, however, was allegedly empirical-theoretical: namely, that latter day psychological research seemed to show that such character traits were domain-specific rather than global; that, in short, agents trained to be honest, brave or self-controlled in this context could be dishonest, cowardly or weak-willed in that one (for classic research of this general drift, see Hartshorne and May 1928). Thus, influenced by a Kantian conception of moral agency—much reinforced by more modern neo-Kantian existentialist and prescriptivist (Hare 1952) perspectives on moral motivation—Kohlberg held that one could expect stable and reliable moral conduct only from agents who had effectively and authentically reasoned (via progress through a series of 'pre-moral' stages of reflection) to consistent or principled moral commitments.

It is clear that Kohlberg's cognitive stage theory of moral development and education was much in tune with the rationalist, liberal-democratic and anti-authoritarian temper of the times—as already noticed, it resonated with other not dissimilar moral educational theories developed outside the US—and that it also dominated the field of moral educational theorizing for several decades. One may also admit that its heart was in the right place in its powerful endorsement of a basic Kantian (Kant 1967) affirmation of the free, rational and responsible character of moral agency. We could not reasonably regard those as morally responsible agents who simply behaved well—however well they behaved—simply because they had been conditioned or indoctrinated so to behave by parents, teachers or some totalitarian authority. Moreover, in the light of another of his key influences—the American pragmatist and educational philosopher John Dewey—Kohlberg attempted important public and practical innovations and reforms through his work on educational 'communities of justice', wherein young people might be taught the social values and virtues of negotiating moral and other differences in a spirit of liberal-democratic and non-violent tolerance, fairness and mutual respect.

With philosophical hindsight, however, one may now see the respects in which the theory was—albeit importantly— off track. It may also be, moreover, that all the less congenial features of Kohlberg's theory stem from its uncompromising neo-Kantian rationalism. So, to begin with, one problem with the exclusive emphasis on the development of moral *rationality* and/or cognition is clearly the age old philosophical difficulty—recognized at least since Plato—of the so-called gap between 'is' and 'ought': that one might well reason to some—however 'true' or 'objective'—conclusion that such and such is the morally right or good course of action without being in the least motivated so to act. Indeed, contemporary empirical psychological research seemed to show that many young people who did appear to reason to this or that moral conclusion in their reflections on Kohlbergian dilemmas could not be relied upon to act accordingly in their day-to-day conduct. In this regard, Kohlberg's theory fared hardly better—if not actually worse —than the 'bag of virtues' views he rejected: just as agents might not always be expected to exhibit a given virtue in all spheres of their lives, so it seemed that there might be shortfall between moral thought and practice in *any* sphere of moral life.

No less seriously, however, the Kantian cost of Kohlberg's moral rationality seemed unreasonably high. In his ethical theory, Kant (1967) suggests that there can be no genuine moral judgement and/or conduct that is not *autonomous*, in the sense of entirely free from the 'heteronomous' demands or constraints of external authority and/or personal motive or inclination: to act morally is to act in obedience to a 'universal' moral law that is entirely above — and invariably at odds with — empirically conditioned human nature, motives and desires. This is an ideal to which Kohlberg's final stage of true justice plainly aspires: despite his work on the social and interpersonal negotiation of moral differences in his 'communities of justice', Kohlberg was not a 'consensus theorist' for whom morality is a matter of social agreement, but an objectivist for whom moral 'right' and 'wrong' are determined by disinterested reason. But much of the drift of modern ethics — from Kohlberg's own time to the present — has been concerned to question any such Kantian ideal of moral reason and judgement as detached or disengaged from the historical, social and personal circumstances that (empirically) condition any and all human agency. While some rational liberty to make moral and other choices is clearly necessary for genuine human agency, it is hard to see how such choices could be made from a position of utter independence of personal and social context — the empirically transcendent 'view from nowhere' — that Kant identifies with rational moral autonomy. To make coherent moral choices is to act from *where we are*, in response to predicaments that are defined by where we are, and which also define *who* we are.

In this light, recent developments in psychology and philosophy have, either explicitly or implicitly, been critical of the general tenor and drift of Kohlbergian thought. To begin with, Kohlberg's account was subject to a notable early broadside from feminist psychologists who argued, on purportedly empirical grounds, that his emphasis on rational principles in moral life did not reflect the moral experience and/or intuitions of women or girls whose moral responses were allegedly shaped more by affect or sentiment than reason. The early objections along these lines of Carole Gilligan (1982) were subsequently developed by Nel Noddings (1983) and others into a more general anti-rationalist moral theory which has since come to be known as 'care ethics'. However, much of the other psychological and philosophical drift away from a Kohlbergian perspective has tended towards reinstatement of the idea of (virtuous) moral character. The first post-war educational attempt to revive the notion of character was made by American psychologists and educational theorists—such as Thomas Lickona (1991) and Kevin Ryan (1995; see also Ryan and Bohlin 1999)—who held that 'academic' Kohlbergian discussion of moral dilemmas could not suffice to produce the dispositions to right conduct that are surely required for full moral agency: in short, young people needed guidance or training not just in moral reflection but also in how to act morally. Still, while these and other early character educationalists made excellent points, much of the wider American character revival was often mired in authoritarian political agendas enshrining rather uncritical and/or crude behavioural conceptions of character. On the other hand, the more recent (also American) movement of so-called 'positive psychology' has sought to develop a more conceptually sophisticated account of character often explicitly drawing on contemporary philosophical revival of Aristotle's virtue ethics—shortly to be considered in this work. However, fairly final proof of a general movement of character to centre stage in contemporary theorizing about moral development and education is that so-called post-Kolhbergians—the first and second generation students and disciples of Kohlberg himself—have almost all now come around to the view that the master's theory needs to accommodate significant reference to the development of virtues of moral character (see, for example, Lapsley and Power 2005).

On the philosophical front, however, the drift towards conceiving moral life and education in terms of character and virtue is commonly dated from the publication of Elizabeth Anscombe's revolutionary paper 'Modern Moral Philosophy' (Anscombe 1981) and clearly precedes any of the just noted psychological developments. In her paper, Anscombe pointed out the shortcomings of the dominant ethical theories of Kantian deontology and utilitarianism of the time and urged a return to Aristotle's virtue ethics as a promising ethical way forward (Aristotle 1941). Basically, Aristotelian virtue ethics takes the view that a virtue is a state of moral character in which various forms of natural human affect, appetite and desire are ruled, shaped or ordered under the guidance of an appropriately developed capacity for rational reflection that Aristotle called *phronesis*, usually translated as 'practical wisdom'. On this view, the moral educational task is to cultivate wise, critical and discriminating dispositions towards—rather than bind or mechanical habits of—honesty, fairness, courage, temperance, benevolence, compassion and other moral conduct. The requirement that such dispositions should be critical and discriminating is crucial. On the Aristotelian view, courage is not a matter of reckless confrontation in any and all circumstances, and generosity is not just foolish liberality: for while there can be little virtue in cowardice or miserliness —where there is too much fear or too little liberality—so there can be little in trivial or pointless antagonism or careless prodigality. It takes the wise judgement of *phronesis* to discern the appropriate *mean* between the various morally undesirable excesses and deficits of affect or sentiment.

That said, recent work in moral philosophy has taken virtue ethics in a bewildering variety of directions—not all of them Aristotelian—so that it is no longer possible to identify any commonly accepted view of virtue or character in contemporary ethics. For present purposes, however, we may distinguish between two very influential versions of the view. The first of these—that we shall here call 'naturalistic virtue ethics'—is closest to the Aristotelian roots of reflection on virtue as character. On this view, variously defended and developed in modern times by Peter Geach (1977), Philippa Foot (1978), Nicholas Dent (1984), Martha Nussbaum (1988, 1995), Rosalind Hursthouse (1999), Julia Annas (2011) and others, a virtue is a *natural* human quality or characteristic insofar as it is generally — and cross-culturally — conducive to human wellbeing or flourishing. From this viewpoint, understanding human nature is crucial to understanding our moral nature: since we would not have the moral concerns we have if we did not also have our evolved biological nature. (Consider, for example, how our reproductive nature shapes our sexual ethics.) However, another more social constructivist or 'anti-realist' virtue ethics — developed and promoted by such philosophers as Alasdair MacIntyre (1981, 1988, 1992) and Charles Taylor (1989) — is rather more sceptical of any such basic human nature. On such 'neo-idealist' views, conceptions of virtue are socially constructed and prone to vary between 'rival' socially constructed moral traditions. Although the present authors — like fellow Jubilee Centre for Character and Virtues colleagues — incline more to the first than the second of these perspectives, the Knightly Virtues project of present concern has also been influenced, as we shall see, by ideas from the second of these views.

The Broader Educational Context

Still, aforementioned developments in academic psychology and philosophy did not occur in splendid isolation, but significantly reflected or echoed the spirit of their times. As already said, Kohlberg's work much reflected the general post-war rejection of totalitarianism and authoritarianism and the corresponding hopes for a brave new world of liberal-democratic freedom, social justice and economic prosperity. However, the character education movement of the late 1980s also evidently mirrored growing public and political unease with or reaction to the more libertarian ramifications — or, in many minds, actual *excesses* — of liberal trends as manifested in the 'sex, drugs and rock and roll' permissivism of the nineteen sixties and seventies. Encouraging the young to make their own authentic choices was one thing, but—as Aristotle had long ago warned—promoting this in the absence of settled states of moral character seemed distinctly more hazardous. In this light, character education began to appear a reasonable moral educational alternative to the theories of Kohlberg and other cognitive developmentalists and such initiatives as *Character Counts* and the *Character Education Partnership* came into being in the USA. Indeed, moral character concerns were evident at the very highest levels of government when President Clinton made reference in his 1997 State of the Union address to character as a national priority for public education, stating that: 'character education must be taught in our schools. We must teach our children to be good citizens.' To be sure, while some American character initiatives have been criticized for their association with conservative political agendas and their adoption of crude behaviour shaping approaches to moral education, the focus on character in many US schools has lately come to the fore—perhaps most notably in KIPP schools[1] which are internationally famous on this score.

While interest in character education has spread beyond the USA—to Australia, Canada and Europe as well as to such Asian countries as China, India, Korea and Malaysia (Singapore has recently adopted a new curriculum called 'Character and Citizenship')—we may for present purposes focus on recent developments in the United Kingdom (UK). Here, with regard to our original question about the very purposes of education, it may be said that there is currently much lively UK debate about whether schools should be priming young people for passing set tests, or preparing them for the unpredictable tests of after-school life. In this regard, the head teachers of such famous independent

---

[1]   http://www.kipp.org

schools as Wellington College and Eton College have both spoken publicly about the need for general school attention to character education. Thus, Anthony Seldon, the head-master at Wellington College, recently stated:

> So should schools prioritise character or exam results? They should prioritise both. Is this a matter for schools or for families? It is a matter for both. Does character matter more at primary school than for secondary school? It matters for both. Why then do I say that schools should prioritise character building above exams? Because if you prioritise exams little or nothing will happen with character. But if you prioritise character, exam success will follow, and for the right reasons. (Seldon 2013)

Moreover, while character education may formerly have been seen as the preserve of faith or independent schools, interest in character has also spread across the wider board of British schooling (see Arthur and Harrison 2014). Such recent 'free schools' as Kings Leadership Academy[2] and Kings Science Academy[3] have placed character education at the top of their educational agendas and have adopted inno-vative approaches to the character development of students. So, for example, Kings Leadership has split the school day into two, focusing on academic subjects in the morning and character development activities in the afternoon. Other schools have attributed much of their recent academic success to wholehearted character development of all pupils. Thus, while Kings Langley school[4] in Hertfordshire was in 2002 placed in the bottom 3% of maintained schools nationally, the school was totally transformed over the next ten years and was this year placed in the top 29% in the country (without equivalences) for GCSE results in virtually

---

[2]   http://www.kingsleadershipacademy.com/
[3]   http://www.kings.ac/
[4]   http://www.kingslangley.herts.sch.uk/

every category. Gary Lewis, head-teacher since 2003, has claimed that while much of this turnaround may be attributed to return to traditional standards—such as the imposition of school uniforms—it was only with explicit introduction of character education that the school and its students really started to improve educationally. A recent *Guardian* newspaper report on the school observed that:

> There aren't many head-teachers who would tell a meeting of prospective parents that it would be fine for their child to get a B grade rather than an A, but Gary Lewis says he has no qualms about doing just that. 'I do it every year,' says the principal of Kings Langley secondary school in Hertfordshire. 'I'm not telling parents I'd be happy with their child getting a B if they were predicted an A. But what I do say is, rather than your child slogging their heart out, I'd prefer it if he or she spent time developing leadership skills or doing charity work, even if that meant not getting a higher grade.' The point is that education isn't all about results. And the strange thing is, says Lewis, he's never had anyone raise an objection. 'Parents get it: they understand how important it is for their children to be rounded individuals with a developed moral compass.'[5]

Other faith and non-faith schools have also deliberately moved in a character education direction. Over the last decade, West Kidlington primary school[6] has gained a national reputation as a 'values-led school'. The school maintains that it is important, not only to teach young people how to get along with one another, but to offer them a vision of good or admirable character and to seek to promote this. The school has developed what it calls a *creative curriculum* to ensure that students develop positive moral and other

---

[5] http://www.theguardian.com/education/2014/mar/11/spiritual-moral-social-cultural-education-schools?CMP=twt_gu

[6] http://www.west-kidlington.oxon.sch.uk/

values in a meaningful and engaging way. Of particular present interest, one might also note that an indicator of the increasing grassroots concern with character education has been the enthusiastic reception by over a hundred British schools of the Birmingham Jubilee Centre's Knightly Virtues programme. In this regard, some schools—such as St Joseph's primary school[7] in Swansea—have actually adopted the eight key virtues of this programme as the virtues for whole school development.

At this point, it may also be noted that other British institutions and agencies besides schools have been concerned with the promotion and practice of character education. One conspicuous example of this is a character and values poster award of several years running promoted by the voluntary organization 'Character Scotland'.[8] This programme aims to encourage young people to explore ideals of character and value through the design of posters. These competitions for 10–18 year-olds encourage young people to reflect on their own character ideals and aspirations in the light of local and global role models and exemplars. This programme, already promoted with enormous success in Scotland, is now being used in schools across England, Wales and Ireland and increasingly across the world. Another British character education initiative is the *Thank You Film Awards*.[9] In this project, young people are encouraged to identify someone to whom they are grateful in their lives and then to make a film about the reasons for their gratitude. Selected films are shown during award ceremonies in Leicester Square, London, Birmingham, Manchester and Glasgow. Voluntary service organizations have also shown growing interest in character education. For

[7]   https://swansea-edunet.gov.uk/en/schools/StJosephsCathedral/ Pages/Default.aspx

[8]   http://www.character-scotland.org.uk/

[9]   http://jubileecentre.ac.uk/456/projects/development-projects/thank-you-film-awards

example, the *Step up to Serve*[10] campaign is concerned not just with recognizing and celebrating the contributions of the young to their communities, but also with researching the character benefits to young people themselves of such contributions. A recent report, *Service Generation* (Birdwell and Millar 2012), has usefully explored the 'double benefit' of volunteering and the extent to which young people are themselves significant beneficiaries of such community service.

Several high profile character-focused reports and publications have also appeared in recent years. In 2010, the British 'think-tank' Demos published a report entitled *The Character Inquiry* (Lexmond and Gist, eds., 2010) which made the case for greater educational and parental attention to character development. In the same year, the report *Of Good Character* (Arthur 2010) presented an overview of research on the state of character education in Britain collected in the course of a series of studies by '*Learning for Life*'.[11] The report concluded that schools can and should teach character and also made suggestions for so doing. More recently, following the riots in England, a commission was established to investigate their possible causes. The ensuing *Riots Commission Report*[12] recommended that each and every school should adopt a policy for character education. Its main recommendation was that more attention to character development might well divert potentially disaffected young people to more constructive use of their talents and energies. The report explicitly advised schools to attend to the task of building character. After the English riots, Prime Minister David Cameron observed that: 'education doesn't just give people the tools to make a good living, it gives

---

[10]   http://www.stepuptoserve.org.uk/
[11]   http://www.learningforlife.org.uk/
[12]   http://webarchive.nationalarchives.gov.uk/20121003195935/http://riotspanel.independent.gov.uk/news/riots-communities-and-victims-panel-reponse-to-home-affairs-select-committee-report/

them the character to live a good life, to be good citizens.' In 2014, the *All Party Parliamentary Group* (APPG) on social mobility advised that the teaching of 'character and resilience' should be an integral part of each and every school's mission and identified a number of schools that sought to teach character as a core component of the curriculum.[13] This commission concluded that such focus on character development might be the best way of breaking the 'glass ceiling' that inhibits social mobility. Again in 2014, a report by the RSA into *Spiritual, Moral, Social and Cultural Education* (SMSCE) entitled *Schools with Soul*[14] suggested that character education should be the lifeblood of schooling by providing young people with the vital resources to cope with the challenges of life. However, the report notes that SMSCE provision is particularly scant beyond the age of 14 because of the pressures of the prevailing examination culture of British secondary schooling.

Further evidence of increasing British interest in character education is provided by a recent *Populus* poll that testifies to wide agreement among parents that schools can and should teach character alongside academic study.[15] The poll found that 87% of parents held that schools should focus on character development and that 95% of parents thought it possible to teach moral values and to form the characters of young people through appropriately designed school lessons, projects or activities. Furthermore, 81% of parents would wish their offspring to be given a clear statement of the values that their school upheld. Again, in addition to David Cameron, other high profile British politicians have recently called for increased attention to character education. For one, the shadow Secretary of State for Education,

---

[13] http://www.appg-socialmobility.org/
[14] http://www.thersa.org/action-research-centre/reports/education/schools-with-soul
[15] http://www.jubileecentre.ac.uk/471/character-education/populus-survey

Tristram Hunt, also advocates the inclusion of character education in schooling:

> Character is not best taught through adversity—its study belongs in the supportive, dedicated and aspirational communities that the best schools provide. Emerging research from people like Professor James Heckman at the University of Chicago and Professor James Arthur at the University of Birmingham clearly demonstrates that character can be taught. What is clear is that this is about more than bolting on some music lessons or sports clubs to the school day. No, this is about learning from the rigorous academic discipline that is character education and implementing a holistic approach that goes beyond extra-curricular activities and into the classroom.[16]

Character, Virtue and the Jubilee Centre for Character and Virtues

On this note, there can be no doubt that the 2012 creation of the University of Birmingham Jubilee Centre for the Study of Character and Virtues greatly reflects this general educational sea change. The Jubilee Centre's aim and vision is to undertake academically and theoretically serious research with a view to the actual practical implementation of the findings of such research in various educational and other institutions and contexts of public life. One of the first publications of the Centre was a *Framework for Character Education* (Jubilee Centre 2013). The *Framework* was developed in consultation with head-teachers, parents, academics, employers and young people in Britain and more widely. This basic statement of the Centre's stance calls for general recognition by parents, policy makers and employers of the educational significance of character education, highlights

---

[16] http://press.labour.org.uk/post/76366667202/schooling-for-the-future-tristram-hunt-speech

the key role of teachers in forming the characters of young people and recommends that schools make clear in their mission statements and elsewhere how they intend to develop the moral character and virtues of their students. To quote a little from the *Framework*:

> Belonging to a school community is a deeply formative experience that helps make students the kinds of persons they become. In a wide sense, character education permeates all subjects, wider school activities and general school ethos; it cultivates the virtues of character associated with common morality and develops students' understanding of what is excellent in diverse spheres of human endeavour. Schools do and should aid students in knowing the good, loving the good and doing the good. Schools should enable students to become good persons and citizens, able to lead good lives, as well as 'successful' persons. Schooling is concerned centrally with the formation of character and benefits from an intentional and planned approach to character development.

So what, then, is character? The above document proceeds to claim that:

> Character is a set of personal traits or dispositions that produce specific moral emotions, inform motivation and guide conduct. Character education is an umbrella term for all explicit and implicit educational activities that help young people develop positive personal strengths called virtues. Character education is more than just a subject. It has a place in the culture and functions of families, classrooms, schools and other institutions. Character education is about helping students grasp what is ethically important in situations and to act for the right reasons, such that they become more autonomous and reflective. Students need to decide wisely the kind of persons they wish to become and to learn to choose between already existing alternatives or to find new ones. In this process, the ultimate aim of character education is the development of good sense or practical

wisdom: the capacity to choose intelligently between alternatives. This capacity involves knowing how to choose the right course of action in difficult situations and it arises gradually out of the experience of making choices and the growth of ethical insight.

In pursuit of such ends and goals, the Jubilee Centre, under the Directorship of Professor James Arthur, has appointed a large staff of researchers from various academic fields relevant to the study of character, including three academic philosophers widely known for their (broadly Aristotelian) work on virtue, character and education. Professor Kristján Kristjánsson, formerly of the University of Iceland and currently director of research in the Jubilee Centre, is author of numerous books and articles on the ethics of virtue; Randall Curren of Rochester University (USA) and author of *Aristotle and the Necessity for Public Virtue* is currently an honorary visiting professor to the Centre; and David Carr, formerly of the University of Edinburgh and author of *Educating the Virtues* (as well as co-author of the present work), is half-time research Professor of Ethics and Education in the Centre. In this guiding philosophical spirit, Professor Kristjánsson (2013) has recently published a paper attempting to dispel some of the myths that have built up around education in virtuous character. For Kristjánsson, the ultimate (Aristotelian) goal of moral character education is to equip students with the intellectual resources for wise liberal-democratic deliberation and choice: thus, on this view, critical thinking is a crucial ingredient in the cultivation of virtuous character. In short, Kristjánsson rebuts any charges that character and virtue require mindless submission to religious, political or other authority and argues that the most compelling of current theories of virtue and character education are framed in a language that is neutral between rival moral ideologies. The team also includes academics from a range of such other disciplines as psychology, education, theology and sociology, ensuring that the study of character and virtue draws on a proper range of research perspectives. That said, given that the Jubilee Centre is centrally concerned with the wider public promotion of virtues of good character for a flourishing civil society —not least in what it takes to be circumstances of some recent neglect of such attention—it is no less dedicated to the development of projects designed to promote practical applications of theoretical reflection and/or research evidence in such contexts as schooling and the professions. In this regard, the Jubilee Knightly Virtues project or present concern may be regarded as just such an example of the application of theory to practice.

Means and Methods of Character Education

However, if a broader education of character and virtue is indeed possible in schools and other contexts, what ways and means might would-be character educators adopt to assist such development—and, indeed, who might such character educators be? Two of the earliest western philosophers to apply their efforts specifically to the problem of character education were Plato and Aristotle, and both of these made observations of enduring value on the issue. For Plato, the education of character or of what he called 'spirit' or resolve had to be more than just an academic education— which might lead a person to lacking adequate strength of will or purpose (Plato 1961)—and he therefore advised the stiffening of character via physical exercise or training and listening to the right kinds of rousing music. However odd these suggestions (especially the latter) may sound, there is no doubt that Plato's ideas had a significant influence on modern western educational institutions—such as British public schools—and on military strategy: educators have often held that character is improved by playing rough games and martial music has often been used on battlefields to stiffen the resolve of troops. That said, it seems that Plato's view of character—which he regarded as a separate psychological faculty from reason or intellect—is limited to those 'executive' virtues as courage or resilience which might assist the wavering soul to stick to its guns under fire.

However, for Aristotle—as lately seen—all candidate virtuous character traits need not just to be under the command of intellect or reason, but actually to *embody* intellect and reason—in the particular form that Aristotle called *phronesis* or practical wisdom—as part of their nature. This is why blindly charging into battle whipped up by the skirl of bagpipes may not count as courage failing proper judgement that such action is appropriate or reasonable. For Aristotle, all virtues of character involve a complex interplay of affect, desire and reason, so that conduct may fall morally short either by excess of appetite or affect—as when the coward is swayed by too much fear—or by its deficit—or when the reckless are foolishly heedless of fear (and hence deficient in good judgement). That said, Aristotle also explicitly held that the ground for moral reason needs preparing in early years by the training of young people in habits of virtuous conduct—even at fairly pre-reflective stages of development—by parents or other guardians who are themselves able to model or exemplify such conduct to the young.

Broadly, then, Aristotle fairly clearly identifies three *loose* conditions (since these may not be, in the practical nature of things, always and everywhere severally necessary or jointly sufficient) for the nurture or formation of virtuous character: affective training in virtuous habits; appropriate parental or other exemplification; and the education of practical reason or wisdom. Still, it should also be noted that these processes are by no means separate and distinct and should certainly not be taken—despite the somewhat contrary impression that Aristotle himself gives in parts of the *Nicomachean Ethics*—to mark discrete stages of development (particularly of the kind often marked by modern developmental theory). To begin with, it should be fairly obvious that—for most good custodians—parental or other moral exemplification will be part and parcel of teaching good moral affect and habit. However, it should also be fairly clear on slightest acquaintance with young children of some linguistic competence that any training in Aristotelian moral habits is also inevitably a matter of the giving of *reasons* for and against a particular course of conduct: it is not as though children at a particular point make some miraculous transition from unreasoning automatons to fully-fledged rational moral agents.

But it seems no less true that the moral exemplification required to assist the progress of the young to moral maturity need not be a matter of the simple unreflective imitation of parental or other custodial conduct. First, like good moral training or habituation, such influence need not be — and probably should not be — unreflective. While young children undoubtedly need to acquire some respect for the reasonable authority of elders, unreflective or uncritical imitation or unswerving obedience to parents, guardians or teachers is not the road to the discriminating judgement of Aristotelian (or other) practical wisdom and surely not to be encouraged by any wise parents, guardians or teachers. From this viewpoint, while such elders should exercise proper authority and discipline over the young, this seems best fostered in a climate of open and critical reflection that allows scope for reasonable disagreement and dissent. But it is also evident that we need not think of moral exemplification purely in terms of the influences on young people of parents, teachers and other mentors, since young people draw moral — or other — inspiration from a wide range and variety of cultural and other sources such as friends, radio, television, film and various forms of literature.

In particular, it cannot be doubted that stories — told to children by parents and teachers from earliest years and subsequently accessed from books, magazines, theatre, cinema, television and other sources — are a prime site and source of young people's knowledge of human conduct and that much of their understanding of moral good and/or ill is formed under the influence of such viewing, listening and reading. Indeed, without pre-empting too much of the main text of this work, it is clear from Aristotle's *Poetics* that the moral educational implications of serious literature were far from lost on this great philosopher—which was at least one significant respect in which he differed from his teacher Plato who could see only the moral downside of literature. However, as we shall shortly see, one of the most compelling modern accounts of the moral educational value of literature is to be found in the otherwise rather un-Aristotelian virtue ethics of Alasdair MacIntyre, and much of the work described in this essay has also drawn inspiration from this direction. At all events, it was largely inspired by such past and present day thoughts on the moral significance and potential of stories that some of the eventual members of the Birmingham Jubilee Centre applied to the John Templeton Foundation for support for a research and development project concerned to promote the moral exploration of stories from classic literature on the part of British school children in the later stages of their primary schooling.

As we shall see, it is no exaggeration to say that the success of this project—judged not least in terms of the over-whelming enthusiasm with which it has been received in the large number of British schools in which it has so far been piloted—has outstripped the wildest hopes and expectations of its original designers. Indeed, the reputation of the Knightly Virtues project has now spread way beyond the shores of island Britain and the programme is now being adopted in its original or other forms in other countries across the globe. It is in the wake of this success story that the present authors have been persuaded of the need for more detailed explanatory location of the Knightly Virtues project in a broader context of educational justification of the moral uses of literature in schools. We may now turn to the detail of this task in the chapters that follow.

Chapter Two

Stories as Moral Knowledge

Ancient and Modern Scepticism about the Value of Stories

It is likely that storytelling has been a definitive feature of human life and association since the dawn of linguistic communication itself, and — in a world in which the 'hard copy' is being rapidly supplanted by various electronic, visual and other vehicles of communication — it remains as deeply embedded in human experience and culture as ever. While it is virtually impossible to conceive of even the most unadorned, impoverished or brutalized childhood as utterly devoid of stories, such narrative fare — in the forms of printed word, performance art or TV and screen movies — clearly also continues to be a rich source of adult recreation, enjoyment and satisfaction. Certainly, the story — in all its forms from fairlytales to popular pulp fiction and cinema to the greatest classics of human creative and imaginative art — has ever been a staple ingredient of formal schooling as well as of the educational life of homes in which nurture has extended beyond the bare minimum of material provision. Indeed, it seems that even the most uncaring, neglectful and abusive homes are seldom devoid of the TV and other distractions that neglectful parents will often substitute for the effort and responsibility of proper parental love, care and attention. For unwanted or neglected children, surrogate attachment to the heroes of TV or video game adventures may sadly be the nearest they come to positive human association or communication.

Still, given the widespread presence of stories in school and other educational contexts, it is worth asking quite what, if any, real *educational* value stories might have for young or old alike. To be sure, it need not be insisted that stories do or should have any educational value as such: it may be that their human value is precisely as sources of entertainment, recreation and/or distraction from the more serious business of life. It may be that the adventures of pulp fiction and cinema or television soap operas, or children's fairytales, do mainly serve to relieve the stress of working life, lighten the heavier academic school-day burdens of pupils or momentarily distract neglected waifs from their otherwise miserable plight. It is also evident that much story and narrative is often so used both within and beyond the formal contexts of schooling. Indeed, leaving aside secondary contexts of explicit English literature teaching, one present author was often struck—as a former supervisor of trainee teachers of some three and a half decades experience—by how seldom stories were employed by (especially primary) teaching students for educational purposes beyond their more instrumental use as opportunities for pupils to improve their literacy skills of reading, comprehension or writing. To be sure, when stories were not used for such instrumental purposes—or to get through the secondary school English literature syllabus—they were most often deployed to provide relief from serious academic study, for entertainment or to keep busy those pupils who had finished the main tasks of the day while their slower classmates caught up.

Moreover, it is likely that neglect of—or perhaps more likely failure to perceive—any deeper educational value or significance in stories, has been reinforced by a powerful latter day prejudice about the nature and sources of humanly worthwhile knowledge. Hence, in the core philosophical discipline known as 'epistemology'—or the theory of knowledge—it has been common to distinguish so-called judgements of *fact* from other kinds of human judgement. This distinction certainly acquired considerable force and authority in the ages of so-called reason and enlightenment (from the seventeenth century onwards) during which western philosophers sought to provide grounds and justification for the new scientific methods that were fast enabling the technological advances of industrial revolution and progress. In this regard, philosophers and theorists of science—particularly those of the influential school of *empiricism*—argued that anything worth regarding as genuine human knowledge needed to be grounded in experimental evidence derived from empirical experience: only on the basis of experimentally reliable and replicable observations could scientists discern the 'natural' laws or regularities upon which the knowledge required for technological progress might be constructed. It was in this light that empiricists were inclined to a sharp distinction between the 'epistemically' reputable judgements of *fact* and the more 'opiniative' judgements of *value*, according to which human moral, aesthetic and expressive discourses could not be rationally justified—if, indeed, they might make any meaningful sense at all. (For the main source of this view, see Hume 1969.) It was also inevitable that this radical empiricist perspective would come to have educational influence and implications —vividly satirized in the words of Dickens' utilitarian schoolmaster Gradgrind: 'Teach these boys and girls nothing but *facts*... you can only form the minds of reasoning animals upon facts: nothing else will ever be of any service to them. Stick to the facts, Sir!' (Dickens 2001, opening paragraph).

Moreover, despite the relatively recent (and, one might also add, *local*) philosophical source of such influence, distinctions broadly similar to that drawn by empiricists between fact and value are of much older provenance and readily discernible in the classical Greek origins of western philosophy—not least, close to present concerns, in the work of its founding father Plato. Thus, while Plato was as far as could be from any kind of empiricism, his political philosophy rests on a conception of knowledge as enquiry into *how things are* — the truth or reality of things — that is positively hostile, more than merely unsympathetic, to what it takes to be the role of creative or imaginative stories in human life and experience. So, while Plato (1961) argues that the world we experience through the senses is itself an unreliable guide to a truth that can only be apprehended by the exercise of pure reason, he nevertheless takes imaginative art and literature — the works of such poets as Homer, Aeschylus and Sophocles — to provide an even more distorted version of the already largely illusory appearances of things. Indeed, for Plato, the artist does not even pretend to depict things as they really are, but tells bare-faced lies about the (non-existent) gods and their squalid antics that serve only to titillate audiences and distract them from any rational appreciation or understanding of right or good conduct. From the outset, artists and poets are deceivers and seducers who, by dint of *rhetoric* rather than reason, are concerned more to please their audiences with sensational stories of unbridled lust and appetite than to reveal genuine knowledge and truth. Plato would have no doubt seen his worst fears confirmed in the average modern pulp fiction or TV soap opera.

In short, Plato draws a distinction between knowledge or truth on the one hand, and fiction on the other, that is not epistemically far removed from the empiricist distinction between fact and value: on both views there are types of human discourse and enquiry defined by appeal to reason, evidence and systematic search for truth that are to be distinguished from those discourses that have more rhetorical, expressive and aesthetic human purposes. Of course, Plato would have disagreed with modern empiricists about much — not least about their dismissal of moral or other value judgements as merely personal or subjective: Plato himself believed that judgements about what is morally right or wrong, good or bad, could certainly be supported or upheld by reason, and—since many (perhaps most) latter day philosophers have sought to defend some sort of moral objectivism—the modern philosophical jury is still certainly out on this question. But there cannot be much doubt that such Platonic, empiricist and similar distinctions have been fatally damaging to any view that imaginative stories might provide routes to knowledge, understanding or insight of much epistemic merit. On these views, imaginative stories may be fodder for entertainment or distraction, but they cannot yield knowledge—to which we should rather look to the hard evidence of science. By this token, empirical— natural and/or social—science has become the modern 'gold-standard' of human knowledge and enquiry and this has been widely reflected in the generally higher status accorded to scientific and mathematical studies in latter day school curricula and in the increasing and corresponding educational marginalization of literature and other arts. In the post-industrial and technological educational contexts of present day society, scientific studies are generally more highly regarded than arts subjects and able students are widely encouraged by politicians, economists and parents to pursue physics, chemistry or mathematics rather than art, music or literature.

To be sure, it may be that bright students are urged or advised to study sciences rather than arts because the former are also regarded as more secure routes to employment and/or of greater social or economic use. From this perspective, however, it would seem that much modern curriculum policy has also inclined to emphasize the *instrumental* or utilitarian merit of any school teaching of literature and the arts, according to which such subjects may be valued in terms of the (commercially and other) useful skills they provide opportunities to acquire and exercise. But such emphasis also bespeaks a certain scepticism or suspension of faith in the actual content of (perhaps especially modern or postmodern) artistic creativity and imagination: it is as though classroom painting, story-writing and music-making has to be justified in terms of the wider utilitarian value of the skills these activities enable, precisely because it is not obvious how one might justify the skills in terms of their creative and imaginative content. Whereas it is easy to see, someone might say, how we may educationally justify the learning of experimental methods in terms of the scientific discoveries to which they may lead that help us better to understand our world, it is less easy to see how we might so defend the learning of skills productive of abstract paintings or imaginative fantasies — unless, of course, these are seen as means to this or that aesthetic decoration or sentimental distraction. In short, the would-be artist is once more — in the spectral shadow of Plato — pointed firmly in the direction of the entertainments industry. Aesthetic effects, on this view, and their effects upon affect — or human sentiment, passion and emotion — are once more consigned to the realm of rhetoric more than intellect, persuasion rather than reason, and have therefore little place in any serious education.

Certainly, there seems to be something amiss with such thinking; but it is of the utmost educational importance to be *precisely* clear about what this is. To be sure, one should not deny that creative literature and other arts are in many if not most cases (with perhaps the exception of some forms of so-called conceptual art) concerned with aesthetic sensibility and emotional response: clearly, literary, visual and musical artworks often aim to *please* and *move* us and are judged as more or less effective, successful or potent in just these terms. In this regard, moreover, it might also make some educational sense to observe a certain *pluralism* about the value of arts: we should not look for or expect to find the same artistic point or satisfaction in a Rubens' portrait as in a Jackson Pollock abstract; in a plainsong chant as in a tenor saxophone solo by Sonny Rollins; or in a Shakespeare sonnet as in a Gunther Grass novel. From this viewpoint — with particular regard to the present focus on narrative literature — it makes sense to observe that not *all* art is concerned with storytelling, and that — respecting a certain modern distinction between 'formalist' and 'expressive' art—we should not expect to appreciate or explain an abstract painting in quite the same way as a novel by Jane Austen. The downside of such argument, however, is that it tends to a no less false distinction between art that is only concerned with pleasing aesthetic effects—pretty arrangements of words, paint or sounds for their own sake—and art in which such arrangements function only as incidental or 'accidental' means to the presentation of a separately identifiable story or narrative. Precisely, it suggests the possibility of fairly sharp distinction between *form* and *content* of artworks—leaving artists free to prioritize one at the expense of the other. But anyone who has ever felt the power of art must find this distinction forced and artificial. The music to Bizet's *Carmen* is not just an accompaniment or ornament to the story of Carmen, it is of the essence of *that* story; the verbal images of Eliot's *The Waste Land* are not distinct from the theme or topic of the poem, they are *constitutive* of it; and the artistic power of Charlie Parker's saxophone playing is not reducible to ingenious arrangement of notes, but is also reflective or expressive of a recognizably human personal and social predicament.

Character, Emotion and the
Moral Significance of Human stories

Following Socrates, Plato appears to have thought that moral virtue is a species of *knowledge* and that knowledge as such was discernible only by the use of pure reason: from this viewpoint, the attempts of poets and other artists to please or move us could only be a distraction from the objective truth of knowledge revealed by reason. However, Plato's no less illustrious pupil Aristotle (1941) took a very different view of the nature of moral virtue, according to which poetry (and/or other art) features as a significant—if not potentially *the* most significant—way in which the nature of virtue might be revealed or comprehended. In a nutshell, this is precisely because Aristotle—unlike Plato—

held that desire, emotion and appetite are no less implicated than reason or rationality in the cultivation or *education* of moral virtue.

To begin with, while Aristotle certainly agrees with Plato that there can be no genuine moral virtue in the absence of reason or rational deliberation—since, as many if not most moral philosophers would agree, a person who does what is right only from blind habit or mechanical conditioning would hardly count as a moral agent—he yet does not regard moral reasoning or deliberation as purely *theoretical* reasoning of the kind in which one might engage in doing science or mathematics. Rather, he regards moral reasoning as a form of *practical* more than theoretical reasoning, to which he gives the name *phronesis* or 'practical wisdom'. Moreover, while such reason is important for determining or deciding the morally right or appropriate thing to do in any circumstances, its primary aim—since, for Aristotle, virtuous conduct has to be motivated in an appropriately virtuous way—is the production or cultivation of morally good *character*: it is only by having a moral or virtuous character that the agent is able to determine the right thing to do and it is the main function of practical reason to form such character. In short, as Aristotle puts it, virtuous or morally right actions can only be understood as the kinds of actions that a morally virtuous person or agent would perform (Aristotle 1941a, book 2, section 6). But does this not, someone might object, rather put the cart before the horse? Do we not first need some standard or rule to determine what counts as a right or good action in order to become moral or virtuous? To be sure, some care is needed here, since Aristotle's ethics does specify criteria of virtuous action and he does indicate that there are certain sorts of action—such as murder, theft and adultery—that are *as a general rule* morally wrong. But the key issue is that at the point of individual and uniquely placed moral decision, there are no absolutely unexceptionable or compelling rules of conduct, so that only good character can determine what is morally appropriate in this or that circumstance. Thus, for example, while the virtuous agent will appreciate that lying is always morally untoward, some measure of dissembling cannot be practically ruled out in circumstances in which telling the truth (to an enemy) may cost many innocent lives (Carr 2003).

But insofar as Aristotelian virtuous character determines what is going to count as morally right action or conduct in any given circumstance, it now needs to be specified how such character may be formed or cultivated. How do agents cultivate the moral virtues of (for example) courage, temperance, justice, honesty, compassion, kindness, generosity and so on, which severally and/or jointly comprise good character? As we have seen, Aristotle departs from Plato: first, in holding that good character cannot be a matter of reason alone; second, in recognizing that human feelings, passions and appetites are not only perfectly proper but actually necessary in their place. Plato (perhaps under Socratic influence) seems to have regarded such emotions as fear, and appetites as sexual desire, as mostly undesirable and unbecoming to rational moral agents: on this view, the courageous would be those who had suppressed or eliminated all feelings of fear and fully rational agents would be above sexual interest or desire. For Aristotle, on the other hand, since fear is a perfectly normal human reaction to threats or dangers, the courageous could not be entirely fearless: indeed, it is not just that it would be unclear why we should *praise* people for courage who felt *no* fear, but that fearlessness in dangerous circumstances looks more like folly than courage. So, for Aristotle, the virtue of courage occupies what he calls a 'mean' or medial position between the excessive fear of cowardice on the one hand and a foolhardy or 'reckless' deficiency of fear on the other. Likewise, since sexual desire has its proper place and function in human life, and it is normal and natural for humans to experience it, the virtue of sexual (or other) temperance occupies a 'mean' position between an 'insensible' deficit of appetite on the one hand and an inappropriate excess of it on the other. Hence, the virtuous ideal of good moral character is generally that of measured or moderate expression of feelings, desires and appetites as circumstances and perhaps (as a rough guide) decent and civilized social conventions dictate.

In this regard, the key role of determining the appropriate mean in any given set of circumstances—how, as Aristotle puts it, to respond appropriately to the right persons or objects, in the right way, in the right place, at the right time and so on (Aristotle 1941, book 2, chapter 6)—is played by the master (intellectual) virtue of *phronesis*: from this viewpoint, Aristotelian moral virtues may be glossed roughly as feelings, emotions and/or appetites ordered in accordance with some deliberative ideal of practical wisdom. But it is crucial to appreciate that, for Aristotle, such 'ordering' is a matter not—as for Plato—of the suppression or elimination of feelings, emotions or appetites, but of their cultivation, refinement or *education*. The truly courageous are those who have learned to put their fears in rational perspective, so that they know when and where it is appropriate (wise, unwise or required) to stand their ground; the truly temperate have cultivated or refined their tastes and appetites so that they are able to enjoy healthy food or drink in nourishing moderation; the generous have learned to give expression to their inclinations to use some of the means or wealth at their disposal to help others, without undue excess or profligacy; and so on for other virtues. The Aristotelian view is that while few of the feelings, passions or appetites to which we are naturally inclined are inevitably negative or destructive in their place—since even anger, fear and envy may play their virtuous parts—such springs of motivation stand in perennial need of re-evaluation and/or adjustment in the light of the practical reflection and deliberations of *phronesis*. Cultivating virtue as character is therefore inevitably a matter of ongoing education of the *emotions*. But how, one may now ask, is such emotional education possible?

Much modern (seventeenth century onwards) philosophy inclined to a psychological distinction between reason
and emotion and/or feeling, or 'cognition' and 'affect'. This
distinction looms large in the work of the Scottish philosopher David Hume who distinguishes passions and emotions that motivate action, but are in themselves rationally
'blind' or devoid of reason, from the reason or intellect that
enable knowledge and understanding of the world but have
no power to move agents to action: as Hume puts it, reason
can only ever be the 'slave of the passions' (Hume 1969,
book 2, part 3, section iii, p. 462). However, more recent
philosophical interest in emotions—from the mid-twentieth
century—has done much to overturn this picture of non-
cognitive emotion and (to a lesser extent) passionless reason,
arguing that it is difficult if not impossible to make sense of
many if not most passions and emotions without some reference to cognitive or rational states. Modern day work has
focused primarily on the so-called 'intentionality' of emotion
—on the cognitive content of emotions or feelings or what
they seem to be *about* (see, for example, Bedford 56–57, de
Sousa 1987, Kenny 1963, Kristjánsson 2007, Mace and Peters
1961–62, Nussbaum 1997, Peters 1972a, 1972b, Solomon
1983, 1988). From this viewpoint, we can only make sense of
fear as a response to some perceived danger or threat; of
anger as a response to injury or insult; of jealousy as per-
ception of attention of significant others to rivals; and so on
for other emotions. To be sure, this point may be—and has
been—somewhat overstated: non-human animals incapable
of reason may be said to feel fear or anger and human emotions are themselves often enough irrational. But it is also
clear that human anger and fear *are* often intentional or
'cognitive' and that there are emotions and passions such as
envy, pride, jealousy, sympathy, pity, compassion, schaden-
freude and so on, that only rational or reasoning creatures
could feel. Moreover, the key present point about emphasis
on the cognitive content of human emotion is that if emotions embody judgements, such judgement may (as in the

case of Othello's jealousy) be *mistaken* as well as correct, and if mistaken be *corrected* — or 'educated'.

This conception of emotions as significantly cognitive or 'intentional' was also clearly anticipated by Aristotle — from whom, to be sure, many latter day theorists of emotion have clearly drawn inspiration (see Kristjánsson 2007). Indeed, Aristotle's view that moral development and/or education is a matter of the cultivation of virtuous character — which, in turn, involves the rational ordering or refinement of feelings and emotions — would be hard to sustain except on an understanding of emotions as involving corrigible or educable perceptions or judgements. In this light, the courageous develop courage not by battling to overcome each and every natural fear, but at least partly by learning to evaluate and distinguish between exaggerated and unfounded threats and dangers which, while perhaps requiring confrontation, may be assessed or faced in more or less sensible ways; the temperate develop emotional self-control not by 'sitting on' their bad tempers but by learning to distinguish significant injustices — where righteous anger may be morally called for — from trivial slights that need not be taken seriously; the truly sympathetic or compassionate require to distinguish between deserving cases of need in which support is merited from those that are less well deserved or more opportunistic; and so on. The general point is that human emotions and passions are not just onslaughts of passive and/or irrational affect that stand in need of dogged resistance or repression, but mindful ways of appreciating, understanding or evaluating the world that may be more or less developed, mature or accurate. From this viewpoint, the emotional problems to which human agents (in fact and fiction) are prone — and the consequent moral problems to which these may give rise — frequently follow from failure to perceive the conduct, intentions and responses of others in a clear and accurate way. To take a familiar literary fictional example, Shakespeare's Othello is not overcome by jealousy as one might be by drink or laughing gas, but is above all *mistaken* about the truth of things. The 'cure' for his jealousy would be to come to see that insinuations of Desdemona's infidelity are unfounded and/or malicious.

But one might now ask what would serve to cultivate or educate human emotions and passions in a morally or virtuously positive or constructive direction? As might be expected, Aristotle, the great ancient master theorist of virtue as character development—and as also, thereby, of the development of emotions—has a number of things to say about this. One key point is that the early development and education of such virtuous character traits as courage, temperance, justice, compassion, sympathy—and thereby of such basic emotions, passions and appetites as fear, anger, sexual desire, self-love or love for others—must involve some basic training in right habits at the hands of parents and other guardians. In this regard, children initially learn to be brave by being encouraged (as a matter of personal 'honour') not to make a fuss at minor scrapes or discomforts; they learn temperance by being encouraged to see the good consequences of self-control and the bad and disagreeable consequences—as well as the personal disgrace—of self-indulgence; they learn to be just or fair by being helped to recognize concern for and responsibility to others rather than brute self-regard as noble and/or praiseworthy conduct; and so on. However, another Aristotelian point, while there is clearly much basic habit training at the heart of such learning, the success of such habituation also much depends on the right sort of examples or guidance that children or young people are given by parents, teachers and other custodians. Clearly, children brought up in circumstances of neglect, or—worse still—abuse, will thereby lack the guidance or example crucial to the proper acquisition of patterns of decent self-respectful and pro-social behaviour. That said, it should be clear that examples of how to live well rather than badly—or, perhaps no less crucially, lessons about the adverse or lamentable consequences of behaving badly rather than well — are clearly available from sources besides such parental or other social contact. In this regard, Aristotle precisely makes much in his *Poetics* (Aristotle 1941b) of the power and potential of imaginative literature for rich insight into moral life and/or virtuous (or vicious) character and — not least — concerning the respects in which human feelings, desires and emotions are implicated, for good or ill, in such character.

As we have seen, Aristotle's illustrious teacher Plato considered the influence of such Greek poets as Homer, Aeschylus and Sophocles to be generally negative or harmful, insofar as their works often depicted divine and human agents engaging in various ignoble or morally disgraceful conduct. The libidinous antics of gods such as Zeus and Aphrodite and the deceitful or downright wicked behaviour of Odysseus or Agamemnon simply set a bad example, thereby encouraging spectators of plays about them to behave likewise. For Aristotle, however, while the characters of Greek tragedy may be taken to provide moral examples, these are not evidently — especially given the sticky ends to which many of them come — examples to be imitated, but warnings of what may happen to us if we are ruled by the violent passions of such agents, or what we may morally become if we are blind to the demands of honesty, decency or justice. In this light, Euripides' tragedy of *Medea* (in which a mother kills her own children) is not to be read as an example to imitate, but rather as an exploration of the lamentable consequences of being ruled by Medea-like passions. However, by virtue of its sympathetic exploration of Medea's predicament as a foreign wife abandoned and betrayed by a heartlessly ambitious Greek husband, Euripides' tragedy also provides an opportunity — as Aristotle's famous doctrine of *catharsis* would seem concerned to emphasize (Aristotle 1941b) — to experience more morally positive and purified human emotions of pity and righteous indignation regarding her wretched plight at the hands of a cruel husband. Likewise, such Euripidean tragedies as *Iphigenia in Aulis* and *The Trojan Woman*, far from celebrating Geek aggression, cruelty and greed (so vividly depicted in these plays) as models to imitate, are evidently concerned to hold up a moral mirror to Greek audiences through which they might examine—by vicarious identification with their local cultural myths and icons—their own actual and potential prejudices, weaknesses and failings. Thus, for example, the wily Odysseus, often celebrated in Greek myth and legend for his wisdom and cunning, is clearly depicted by Euripides as an unscrupulous, treacherous and malicious rogue whom no one of the slightest moral scruple or integrity could really wish to be. At all events, in sharp contrast to Plato—whose only educational use for poetry or other rhetoric was in the service of state propaganda—Aristotle clearly regards such appeals to passion and emotion as of much potential moral educational value. In short while Plato condemned poetry on account of its rhetorical and emotional content, Aristotle—for whom well-ordered feeling and emotion are the very stuff of character development—precisely recognized the enormous potential for emotional education of poetry and (at least by implication) other arts.

Indeed, more generally, it would seem that the stories and narratives with which much Greek poetry and literature dealt were morally—and hence moral educationally—significant for Aristotle because they are the main vehicle of our understanding of human purpose, motive and agency. To be sure, on a theoretical level, Aristotle adopts a naturalistic—quasi-biological—approach to the study of ethics in which the moral dispositions of human virtues are regarded as functionally conducive to human wellbeing or flourishing (*eudaemonia*): on this view, the moral virtues are qualities that enable us to do well as members of a biological species—and therefore (as a more recent Aristotelian has put it): 'men need virtues as bees need stings' (Geach 1976, p. 17). On the other hand, however, insofar as moral and other human agency is also a matter of peculiarly human rational motive, intention, desire, practical deliberation and action, there can be no full understanding of moral life entirely in terms of the causal explanations of natural science, and such life, agency and associations seem to call for narrative construal. As earlier indicated, in the wake of post-war neo-Aristotelian action theory, the influential contemporary British moral and social philosopher Alasdair MacIntyre (1981, 1988, 1992) has recently defended — against any and all forms of natural and social scientific reductivism — an influential modern *teleological* conception of moral and other human agency. On this view, understanding self and identity is not a matter of establishing the conditions of human physical or even psychological continuity, but of grasping the roles played by individuals in *narratives* that others tell about them or that they tell about themselves. For MacIntyre, the unity of the human person is explicitly the unity of a *character* in one or more *stories*, in which any and all human actions are constitutively implicated. Apart from such narratives, MacIntyre maintains, it is all but impossible to individuate or make sense of human persons and/or their conduct at all. It is also clear from MacIntyre's account that evaluation of persons and their conduct is essentially normative or *moral*, and that it has thereby significant affective and volitional constituents and dimensions. But above all, on this view, it seems that stories provide *knowledge* and insight of the highest human importance — because, without them, we cannot as human agents understand *ourselves*.

Chapter Three

Approaches to and Uses of Stories for Character Education

Preamble

While it is the main concern of this chapter to explore the possibilities and prospects of the use of literature for moral or character education, it is not here claimed that this is its *only* legitimate educational use: clearly, not all creative and imaginative literature has narrative content, and a good deal of it of it—like much other artwork of painting, music and dance—aims to enchant and delight through aesthetic effect, or to challenge and stimulate via ingenuity of technical construction or design. As previously noted, lyrical, dada or other poetry may have little or no narrative content and there seem to be literary works of narrative construction— such as (at least arguably) James Joyce's *Ulysses* or Samuel Beckett's *Krapp's Last Tape*—wherein the exploration of moral themes or the study of moral character may not be of paramount concern. Still, in the spirit of Aristotle and Alasdair MacIntyre, it would appear that a broad spectrum of literary narrative—including various cultural (religious and other) myths, legends and folklore, poetry and drama, works of imaginative fictional and other literature—invites understanding as concerned to explore broadly moral themes of human meaning and purpose, to raise key questions about the proper direction of human agency and about what sort of persons, in terms of the development and exercise of virtuous qualities of character, human agents might or should aspire to become. In this light, indeed, we might here first broadly distinguish those large literary and other artistic canvasses that seem more or less definitive of major moral and other cultural ideals, from those more particular literary or other artistic studies or explorations of individual moral aspiration and struggle to achieve, realize or even resist such ideals.

In terms of this rough distinction, the roots of present day Anglophone culture — if not of western culture generally — are often located in the Bible and Shakespeare. To be sure, insofar as it is not hard think of other literary sources (such as Homer's *Iliad* and *Odyssey*, Virgil's *Aeneid*, Ovid's *Metamorphosis*), and authors (such as Aeschylus, Sophocles, Euripides, Malory, Dante, Milton, Cervantes) who have hardly less significantly contributed to the development of western educated sensibility, this may seem more a comment on literary influences upon more local development of the English language than upon the cultural and intellectual constitution and character of western thought as such. There can be little doubt that the King James version of the Bible had enormous influence on the subsequent shaping of ordinary modern idiomatic English and it has been frequently quipped that the trouble with Shakespeare's plays is that they are full of quotations — reflecting (at the risk of spoiling a joke by explaining it) the widespread and seamless weaving of Shakespearean references and/or quotes into modern English usage. Still, with regard to the form more than the content of these works, the Bible — as the key source of the theological, moral and political ideas and ideals that have shaped much of western society — mainly falls on one side of our distinction; and Shakespeare — as a time-honoured source of studies of individual characters struggling, often against their own inner conflicted natures, to live worthwhile or fulfilled human lives in accordance with or in defiance of such ideals — seems to fall mainly, along with so much Greek tragedy and later imaginative English, European and American western drama and fiction, on the other side of it.

Virtue and Literature:
Narratives of Human Purpose and Destiny

With regard to the first arm of this distinction, the Christian Bible seems definitive of modern western culture in much the same way that the Qur'an is of Islamic culture or the Upanishads and Mahabharata are of Hindu culture. However, given its generally religious and more specifically theistic commitments, the Bible—and, more especially, any public (educational or other) teaching of the Bible—has clearly become extremely contentious in the modern liberal democracies that have historically emerged from western Christendom. As indicated in our introduction, the promotion of Christian religious education in state schools has been widely regarded—at least since the Second World War—as at least *sociologically* problematic in view of large-scale migration from non-Christian societies and cultures to Britain and many other western European countries. For many, it has seemed culturally imperialist—just a further perpetration of western European colonial injustice—to impose teaching of or about the Christian religion in schools in which the majority of pupils may be Muslims or Hindus. This, it should be said, has been a particular issue for state education in the United Kingdom, insofar as Britain—unlike the US and also other European countries which preserved state school secularity as one key aspect of the separation of church and state—continued, well into post-WWII years, to support a quasi-confessional (if also often half-hearted) religious educational function for British schooling. Thus, as earlier noted, the British 1944 Education Act famously required a 'daily act of worship' in British state schools, in which—as one present author can verify from personal experience—pupils were required to pray and sing hymns of praise to the God of Christian faith and practice. However, while such unreconstructed Christian confessionalism has now largely (and in the present view quite rightly) disappeared from British state schools, one trouble with its widespread replacement by a religious education based more on teaching about the cultural and other practices of different faiths — presumably in the interests of inter-cultural dialogue, cooperation and respect — is that this also seems to have led to some neglect of substantial and meaningful teaching of biblical or other religious literature and stories.

To be sure, perhaps the most powerful modern objection to any religious or other instruction in biblical (or Qur'anic or Hindu) narratives is that these cannot be taken to represent *educationally* worthwhile or epistemically credible sources of knowledge: at best, insofar as they do not much look like any sort of truth; at worst, because they seem — taken literally — demonstrably false. In this regard, from at least the nineteenth century, an academically reputable tradition or industry of modern biblical criticism has cast serious doubt on the purported historicity of many if not most Old and New Testament narratives. In this light, compelling historical doubts have been raised about the actual existence of many if not most Old Testament characters (such as Abraham, Moses and David) — and, consequently, about the historical veracity of any events in which such agents are alleged to have been implicated — and the different Gospel accounts of the comings and goings of Jesus have been shown to be (in addition to empirically implausible) mutually inconsistent, as well as wildly at odds with the non-canonical gospels discovered at Nag Hammadi and also known from other sources. On this score, we cannot safely treat the biblical narratives of the Jewish exodus from Egypt, David's slaying of Goliath or Jesus's raising of Lazarus as reliable historical events. In the last resort, of course, the core complaint of this kind against the epistemic credibility of biblical (or other religious) narrative is based on a deep secular liberal skepticism — grounded in largely empiricist doubts about the possibility of any knowledge of God or His existence—traceable to such enlightenment philosophers as Hume and Kant. Indeed, for a highly vociferous (and often distinguished) lobby of contemporary militant atheists, it is not just that we can have no knowledge of the existence of God, but that the very idea of God can make little or no *sense* —and that, to boot, the cruelty and carnage that has been historically wrought in the name of tribal loyalties to such non-existent deities is more than enough reason to dispense with such incoherent nonsense. From this stark perspective, there can be little or no justification for educational instruction in biblical narratives in state (or other) contexts of schooling.

To be sure, leaving aside the anti-religious bigotry that has sometimes underpinned such criticisms, there is no doubt something in them. For one thing, from a moral and/ or political (or at least liberal-democratic) viewpoint, it seems that according higher status to one religion over others in contexts of religious or other education—especially in (British or other) multicultural contents—is no longer tenable. On top of this objection, however, any confessional teaching of religious knowledge or education would seem highly problematic. Whether or not one takes this or that particular religious claim to be true—or to merit the status of knowledge—such claims are hardly susceptible of the same *a priori* or empirically grounded proof or evidence as mathematical, scientific or historical statements. Of course, people are no less at liberty to deny that '2 + 2 = 4', that humans and apes had a common ancestor or that the Allies won the Second World War than they are to deny that God is three persons: but it is no less evident that the contestable theological nature of this last claim could hardly command the general (if not quite universal) assent that assures some educational warrant for the other three. As modern theorists of knowledge and science have indicated, there are fairly objective criteria—logical proofs or empirical tests—to which all those inclined to defend or deny the truth of these three claims might appeal in cases of serious dispute: such claims are at least credible *candidates* for knowledge, not so much because they are verifiable, but because they are at least in principle—as it has been said—*falsifiable* (Popper 2002). But while the claim that there is a God and that He comprises three persons may fit coherently into some particular theological perspective, there are no such objective or shared criteria or tests—even in principle—that would settle the matter in favour or against apostasy from this view. Thus, for purposes of public education, such claims—even if *true*—could not count as more than the partisan and dubious opinions of individuals or local communities of faith.

Still, *all* this may be granted without it supporting any case whatsoever against the teaching of (Christian or other) religious *narratives* in schools. Indeed, while the recently rehearsed arguments are telling against *confessional* approaches to religious education (in which religious doctrines or stories are taught as true or to be believed) and/or against any *preferential* teaching of some particular (the locally dominant) religious faith, they are clearly not decisive against religious education *as such,* and they are already effectively rebutted by non-confessional approaches to RE which precisely do *not* regard any given religion as true or as superior to others. In this regard, while teachers need not deny the special religious significance that some cultural narratives have for some particular faith communities, they are clearly free to teach—consistently with the claims of modern biblical scholarship about many biblical narratives —that: the *Genesis* story of Adam and Eve is better understood as a moral and spiritual tale than as a rival scientific hypothesis (to evolutionary theory) about human origins; that the *Exodus* story of the release of the Jews from Egyptian captivity also celebrates—perhaps more in figurative than literal terms—the experiences of suffering and hope of an oppressed people; and/or that—while we need not deny that the New Testament narratives may have historical basis in the lives of Jesus, Paul and the Christian apostles—their highest significance may also lie in the moral and spiritual

lessons that the parabolic and other more figurative adorn-
ments of the Christian story are clearly at most pains to
illustrate. Hence, from a serious educational viewpoint, we
might rediscover the spiritual baby in the bathwater of much
traditional religious education in those great cultural narratives that often seem to have fallen by the wayside—in
different ways and for different reasons—in *both* confessional and non-confessional approaches to religious education (see Carr 2007).

To be sure, it cannot be too much repeated or empha-
sized that to locate the educational import of Christian biblical narratives—until recently regarded as well nigh constitutive of western educated sensibility—in their allegorical or
figurative more than literal or 'factual' significance is *not* to
deny or belittle their *religious, spiritual, moral* or other truth:
on the contrary, it is to affirm it in the highest terms. At this
level alone—irrespective of and notwithstanding any special
regard or priority that one might give to such texts as definitive of one's own identity or faith community—it is to rank
(for example) *Genesis, Job, Ezekiel, St John's Gospel, Acts* and
Revelations alongside the great narratives of Greek and
Roman antiquity as celebrated in the poetry of Homer,
Aeschylus, Sophocles, Euripides, Virgil, Ovid and others
rightly regarded as formative of western educated sense and
sensibility. From this viewpoint, indeed, to argue from the
perspective of dogmatic and bigoted atheism that the evident (empirical) falsity of biblical narratives undermines
their educational value is no less misguided, myopic and
philistine than to argue from some religious perspective that
Homer and Virgil can have little or no (spiritual, moral or
other) educational merit because their works, unlike those of
the Bible, are not *true*. What both the anti-religious and the
'religious' responses here share is a common failure to comprehend wherein the truth and significance of such great
narratives lies. To be sure, it may be somewhat misleading to
regard the profound attempts to understand relations
between freedom and responsibility that we encounter in

both *Genesis* and Aeschylus's *Prometheus Unbound* as 'truths' in the common fact-stating sense of this term (especially insofar as they seem to offer rather conflicting perspectives on this issue): but they are both clearly sources of wisdom and insight into the deepest human concerns and problems of meaning and value of the highest philosophical and cultural importance.

Moreover, it should be clear that both the books of the Christian bible and the works of Homer and Virgil are prime sources and forerunners of such later canonical western literary works as Ovid's *Metamorphosis*, Dante's *Divine Comedy*, Milton's *Paradise Lost*, John Bunyan's *The Pilgrim's Progress*, Christopher Marlowe's *Doctor Faustus*, Shakespeare's *Troilus and Cressida*, Lord Byron's *Prometheus*, Percy Shelley's *Prometheus Unbound*, Goethe's *Faust*, James Joyce's *Ulysses*, Thomas Mann's *Dr Faustus* and *Joseph and his Brothers* and any number of other literary masterpieces that have drawn on or otherwise referred to classical (Greek and Roman) and/or biblical sources. However, even where they have not been concerned with direct reworking of biblical and classical themes, it is clearly all but impossible to understand the flower of the western literary canon without significant acquaintance with its biblical and classical roots. Again, examples could be endlessly multiplied, but it would evidently be difficult for readers to make much sense of the theology, philosophy and references of (for example) Shakespeare's *Hamlet*, Keats' *Nebuchadnezzar's Dream*, Dickens' *Christmas Carol*, Matthew Arnold's *Dover Beach*, W.B. Yeats' *Adam's Curse*, T.S. Eliot's *The Waste Land*, Graham Greene's *Brighton Rock*, Samuel Beckett's *Eh Joe*, Albert Camus's *The Myth of Sisyphus* or C.S. Lewis's *Narnia* stories without some basic acquaintance with their biblical and/or classical sources or inspirations. Like it or not, much if not most significant western literature is directly or indirectly inspired or informed by such biblical and classical sources and/or shot through with allusions or references to them, ignorance of which is likely to render readers bereft of much capacity to comprehend such works: from this viewpoint, it is not just people of faith who would stand to be culturally disinherited by any secularizing effort to deny access to bible stories or classical myths in the education of schooling, but *atheists* as well—and there is already evidence that, for various reasons, such cultural disinheritance is widely occurring in contemporary schools.

Moreover, it should be clear that classical and biblical narratives do also continue to raise and address—in extraordinarily striking and compelling ways—fundamental spiritual, moral and political problems about the human condition and the very meaning of human life and association of a kind to which any and all serious subsequent literature would be hard put to avoid returning. As already noted, such themes—particularly those of relations between authority, freedom and responsibility—are the focus of both *Genesis* and the Greek myth, notably reworked by Aeschylus, of the rebel titan Prometheus. (Indeed, it is more than likely that Aeschylus was drawn to the myth of Prometheus because—as a veteran of Greek resistance to the menace of Persian tyranny—he was precisely interested in the question of political tensions between authority and freedom.) But much the same issues are also evidently to the fore of John Milton's *Paradise Lost* in the morally, spiritually and religiously ambivalent portrait of Satan who combines features of both heroic Promethean resistance fighter and foul Christian villain. Indeed, the other key theme of *Paradise Lost*—following that of the expulsion of the rebel angels from heaven and their consignment to hell—is the *Genesis* story of Satanic corruption of the biblical parents of mankind which is also concerned with fundamental issues of authority, freedom and the place of obedience in human association. It is also clear that *Genesis* offers stark diagnosis of the consequences of disobedience to divine command (or perhaps ecclesiastical law, civil authority or received tradition)—of a sort that many of reform or romantic temper would later come to see as having seriously blighted

Christian theology and tradition. From this viewpoint, it is noteworthy that the *Genesis* story had a much more complex meaning in the theology of early Gnostic and other Christians for whom the fall from innocence into the knowledge of (even adverse and painful) experience needed to be viewed as an indispensable and inevitable means (the Christian *felix culpa*) to the final redemptive salvation of full human growth and maturity. Testifying to the perennial nature of the theme, the 1998 movie *Pleasantville* may be seen as a compelling and entertaining Gnostic reading of this *Genesis* theme.

Virtue and Literature:
The Anatomy of Human Character

Still, while the epic narratives of the Bible and classical Greek myth clearly raise issues of large moral and spiritual significance concerning the meaning and purpose of human life, it seems that the main actors in these stories — such as Adam and Eve, Satan, Prometheus, Faust and Christian (in *Pilgrim's Progress*) — are seldom well-drawn or lifelike characters and that they play more symbolic or allegorical roles in such larger religious or philosophical dramas. To this extent, they are human cyphers or variables, those 'every-persons' with whom we can all identify, but who have (perhaps beyond a specific gender) no very particular human face. However, it is distinctive of an Aristotelian ethics of virtue and character that problems of moral life and association have very particular and distinctive human faces: the moral issues and problems in which human agency is implicated are in fact more or less unique to the precise historical circumstances in which they arise and to the specific human personalities and characters thrown together in such circumstances. Insofar, one may be hard put to learn much of substance or worth about the nature of human moral association or interaction from highly abstract moral theories — of the kind, perhaps, canvassed in modern times by the ethics of duty and utility — and this seems to be precisely

why Aristotle insisted that the moral understanding of practical wisdom (*phronesis*) above all requires protracted experience of the variable rough and tumble of practical human
life. Moral wisdom, in short, is best learned from experience.
That said, it does not seem that Aristotle was what would
nowadays be called a moral 'particularist' — that is, someone
who denies that there can ever be much in the nature of
moral *rules* identifying forms of conduct that are always
morally right or virtuous and which are to be obeyed without exception (for example, Dancy 2004; also Hooker and
Little 2001). On the contrary, Aristotle at one point (Aristotle
1941a, book 2, section 6) says that that there can be no
deliberating about when, where and with whom to commit
murder, theft or adultery — since these could never be
morally good or virtuously chosen forms of conduct. Still,
we have also seen that Aristotle regarded such ideal types of
moral virtue as honesty, courage and fairness as particularly
— albeit imperfectly — exemplified in the diverse actions of
agents in variable human circumstances. Thus, while Plato
may have been right to think that there are no perfect
instances of justice, courage, temperance and wisdom to be
found in the vale of human imperfection, Aristotle may be
no less right to suppose that we might still recognize and
learn from available examples of human aspiration to such
virtuous ideals.

Indeed, as already noted, Aristotle explicitly held that the
past and contemporary literary works (epic, tragic or comic)
of his own culture — of Homer, Aeschylus, Sophocles,
Euripides, Aristophanes and others — could greatly serve to
teach spectators, readers or audiences about the moral complexity of such aspirations and/or about human failure or
(at least partial) success in achieving them. To be sure, while
the dramatic narratives of Greek tragedy are clearly fictional
constructs that should not be taken to depict the actions of
real-life (divine or human) agents, they may nevertheless
enable imaginative exploration of general or archetypal
features and problems of human moral engagement that few

humans would have much trouble recognizing or relating to. In this regard, it is much to the purpose of poetic narratives that the despair of Oedipus, the jealousy of Othello or the struggle for justice of an Antigone is not the particular emotion or passion of this particular agent, but—in a significant sense—the emotional response that 'every-person' might well feel in the circumstances. Aristotle captures this point in his *Poetics* by observing that: poetry 'is something more philosophic and of graver import than history', since it is addressed to matters of *universal* more than particular human concern (Aristotle 1941b, chapter 9). Thus, unlike historians, literary artists are not primarily concerned, if at all, to report, record or inform us of the passing of this or that event, but rather to express or communicate with all the imaginative and creative resources at their disposal the affective, moral or spiritual significance of an experience or event: thus, for example, a Wilfred Owen war poem does not aim to tell us that such and such an event occurred, but to help us experience (via images of the physical and moral horror of war) what it must have been like to be there. Moreover, in Aristotle's famous—albeit evasive—discussion in his *Poetics* of the process of 'catharsis', it seems to be suggested that the value of great tragic poetry—through its moving exploration of the moral consequences of powerful (but often misplaced) emotion and motive—lies in its potential for the refinement or education of the spectator's emotions. In this regard, for example, we may well learn much of moral consequence for our own emotional lives—that is, about the need for wise evaluation and moderation of potentially destructive affect—from the intense dramatic encounter with Othello's jealousy.

Arguably, then, much literary narrative is evidently concerned with close study of the affective, emotional and motivational dimensions of human life—as these figure, for good or ill, in human character—and with the moral issues and dilemmas in which such aspects of character are invariably and inevitably implicated. Again, while we need not pause here for any comprehensive inventory of past and present works of which this seems to be true, it may be worth dwelling briefly on a few choice examples.

As already noted, Greek tragedy offers some of the best ever explorations of the moral implications and consequences of flawed human character—of, precisely, how human agents with good, bad or indifferent character cope or bear up in the teeth of misfortune or adversity. In his *Poetics*, Aristotle quotes Sophocles as saying that 'he (Sophocles) drew men as they ought to be, Euripides as they are' (Aristotle 1941b, chapter 25, 1460b 35). Certainly Euripides, who Aristotle evidently admired, seems to have excelled in portraits of the anti-hero, and—perhaps especially—'wicked' women. That said, as previously indicated, many of Euripides' female characters seem also to be studies of extreme nobility in the face of immense tribulation and suffering. This is particularly true of his dramas focused on Homeric themes of Greek-Trojan conflict—such as *Iphigenia at Aulis* and *The Trojan Women*—wherein almost all the women (with the exception of the vain and selfish Helen) behave heroically at moments of extreme duress: whereas Iphigenia, daughter of King Agamemnon, faces sacrifice to the sea god Poseidon in order to secure favourable winds to carry the Greek fleet to Troy, the captive Trojan women— following the fall of Troy—face humiliation, bondage and ultimate violation at the hands of their brutal Greek captors, who also murder the infant son of Hector's widow to forestall possible future revenge from the grown child. On the other hand, the male actors in these tragedies—those great heroes of Homeric legend and of Euripides' own Greek cultural heritage—are portrayed (with the notable exception of Achilles—otherwise often prone to bad press in Greek drama) as the very worst scoundrels. The Greek commanders-in-chief of the Trojan expedition, namely Agamemnon and his brother Menelaus (whose wife Helen, by her adultery and elopement with the Trojan Paris, has caused the conflict) are portrayed as weak, cowardly and irresolute and, perhaps more surprisingly, Odysseus — the archetypal brave and cunning hero of Homeric legend — is depicted in both dramas as treacherous, manipulative and cruel. But in blackening the characters of the iconic heroes of Greek legend and exalting the virtues of the defeated legendary enemies of Greece — rather than the other way around — Euripides' moral purpose could not be clearer: that it is the audience and those with whom they might culturally identify who stand in most need of moral self-examination. In New Testament spiritual terms, the moral task is to cast the beam from out of one's own eye, before removing the mote from someone else's.

Much the same general points may be made of Euripides' touching portrayal of Medea in his tragedy of this title. The character of Medea features in the Greek myth of Jason and the Argonauts in which the Greek (or Hellene) hero Jason sails off (in the company of Hercules, Orpheus and other classical Greek luminaries) to the kingdom of Colchis to purloin the legendary Golden Fleece, nailed to a tree guarded by a dragon. After many adventures along the way, Jason undergoes and passes a number of tests and challenges set for him by the King of Colchis (and intended to ensure his demise) and eventually manages to steal the fleece despite the king's best efforts to prevent him. In all of this he is aided and abetted by the king's daughter Medea, who has fallen in love with Jason. Medea is also a priestess of the dark witch goddess Hecate and something of a sorceress. Moreover, when the Argonauts are pursued by a Colchean fleet bent on revenge, Medea — who has eloped with Jason — shows her dark side by slaying her own brother, dismembering his body and throwing the butchered parts overboard into the sea. This succeeds in delaying the Colchean pursuit while the murdered boy's father collects the body parts for proper burial. However, following the Argonauts' return home and his fathering of two sons by Medea, Jason deserts her for a more politically advantageous union with Glauce, daughter of Creon, King of Corinth. In a fit of crazed and vengeful fury at Jason's betrayal, Medea then proceeds to slay her own children. Thus, in terms of the received narrative, Medea has an exceptionally bad press in Greek mythology and is clearly taken to typify the treacherous, malevolent and cruel foreign vixen, servant of the barbaric oriental goddesses of night and sorcery and enemy of all things rational, civilized and Hellenistic. In some contrast to this, however, Euripides' moving portrayal of Medea as a would-be loyal wife and mother deeply wronged by an unscrupulously ambitious and unfeeling *Greek* husband is the very soul of understanding and compassion. Medea's predicament—including the despair and anguish that drives her to infanticide—is sympathetically explored by Euripides as the emotional condition that any woman, Greek or foreign, might be expected to feel in the circumstances.

However, another time-honoured literary source of study of human character is of course provided by the impressive dramatic corpus of Shakespeare. Like the poetic dramas of the great Greek tragedians, Shakespeare's plays—comedies, histories and 'problem plays' no less than tragedies— abound with profound and insightful explorations of the moral consequences, for good or ill, of various virtuous and/or vicious character types. Again, while Shakespearean tragedy is also not short of wicked women—such as Lady Macbeth, Goneril and Regan—it seems, as in much Greek tragedy, to be the *virtues* more than the vices of Shakespearean heroines that shine forth in the largely benighted world of patriarchal oppression, masculine vanity, misplaced ambition and general male folly. For the most part, Shakespearean heroines such as Cordelia, Portia, Hermione, Viola and Desdemona are morally and spiritually healing and redemptive figures, not least when they pay the ultimate penalties of humiliation, rejection or death at the hands of foolish men. Thus, while the Juliet of Shakespeare's romantic tragedy is no less of a star-struck and star-crossed lover than Romeo, she has evidently more of a head on her young shoulders and is much less prone to the narcissistic illusion and folly of Romeo—or of other posturing champions of male honour codes. Again, in *The Merchant of Venice* —despite her absurd comic disguises and ruses—it is the basic good horse sense and judgement of Portia that far outshines the folly and racism of Antonio and the poisonous malice of Shylock (not to mention the idiocy of her father in casting her matrimonial prospects to the winds of arbitrary choice of one of three caskets). But it is a notable feature of the day-saving wit and practical wisdom of Portia that it seems entirely devoid of the clouded passions of race prejudice and desire for revenge that equally disfigure the judgements of Antonio (whose haughtiness and contempt render him reckless) and Shylock (who has allowed suffering to poison his soul).

Still, it is arguably the classic Shakespearean tragedies— *Macbeth*, *Othello*, *King Lear* and *Hamlet*—that provide the most serious and sustained studies of the moral implications of human character or, more precisely, of the respects in which moral corruption or failure of character can wreak havoc in human affairs. In *Macbeth* and *Othello*, the leading actors set foot upon the stage as men of considerable virtue and courage who have both distinguished themselves as loyal servants of their lawful masters and resident states. From thereon, however, we are witness to a dismal spectacle of moral decline—by dint of a lethal cocktail of personal flaw and malign influence—into the delusion and death that mark the careers of all such tragic heroes from classical Greek drama onwards. Macbeth's flaw is a flame of personal ambition that—under the poisonous influence of his wife— he fans into an all-consuming and remorseless passion. Othello's flaw (replicated, with slightly less dire consequences, by Leontes in *The Winter's Tale*) is an equally lethal cocktail of overblown sexual passion, male possessiveness and lack of trust, no less fanned into self- and other-destructive jealousy by the scheming and malign Iago. In both plays, Shakespeare artfully traces the steps by which these anti-heroes are drawn deeper into psychological pits and traps of self-delusion and betrayal from which any final extrication and redemption proves impossible. On the other hand, while it is other characters — such as the murdered Duncan, Banquo and Desdemona — who are more conspicuous victims of Macbeth and Othello, it seems to be King Lear himself who is the ultimate casualty of his own lack of maturity and wisdom. Lear is evidently prey to the false consciousness of all in positions of power in taking the flattery of all those under his command as a sign of genuine loyalty and love. Thus, when those such as Cordelia and Kent who genuinely do love him try to bring him to some honest recognition of the truth, he is unable to accept this and reacts — with ultimately destructive consequences to self, others and state — with the tantrum of a spoiled toddler.

While the moral problem raised by *Hamlet* is of a rather different kind from those of the other major Shakespearean tragedies, this play seems of no less significance for understanding the moral dimensions of human character. As we have seen, in the classic Aristotelian account, moral virtue is a matter of appropriate ordering or adjudication of appetite and affect in the light of practical wisdom. From this viewpoint, we may want to say that the trouble alike with Macbeth, Othello and Lear is that they allowed themselves to be ruled by disordered feelings or passions and did not sufficiently think through their emotional obsessions or distorted values to (fairly obvious) correct conduct. In short, we might say that they did not reflect *enough*. On the other hand, *Hamlet* has been described as 'the tragedy of a man who could not make up his mind'. And the reason why Hamlet seems unable to make up his mind may not be that he does not think enough but that he thinks *too much*. The problem for Hamlet, as this character himself puts it in his most famous soliloquy, is the tendency of 'the native hue of resolution' to be 'sicklied over by the pale cast of thought' (Shakespeare 1971, act 3, scene 1, lines 84–85). To be sure, there are intimations in the play of obsession and/or clouded passion on Hamlet's part. Thus, in the context of the hero's hostility to Claudius, the ghostly visions of Hamlet's father are open to Freudian 'oedipal' interpretation—and may at least be meant to raise some doubt in the minds of audiences about the objectivity of any evidence for the murder of Hamlet senior by his brother. Irrespective, however, the play seems squarely focused on the familiar human difficulty of what is to be done in any circumstance where the best evidence points to conflicting possibilities of resolution: precisely, 'whether 'tis nobler in the mind to suffer the slings and arrows of outrageous fortune, or to take up arms against a sea of troubles and by opposing end them' (Shakespeare 1971, act 3, scene 1, lines 57–60). So it may be the key lesson of *Hamlet* for any study of virtuous character as wise deliberation is that of whether there might be non-virtuous excess of reflection and deliberation, no less than non-virtuous excess of affect or appetite.

While the classic heroes, heroines, villains and vixens of Shakespeare and Greek drama have lost none of their power —when evocatively staged or taught—to capture the imagination of both young and old, it is perhaps in the modern novels of late eighteenth- and nineteenth-century writers that the close study of character in more familiar, albeit highly romanticized, domestic contexts and settings comes into its own. Notably, many of these novels, such as Jane Austen's *Sense and Sensibility*, *Pride and Prejudice* and *Emma*, Charlotte Bronte's *Jane Eyre*, Emily Bronte's *Wuthering Heights*, Anne Bronte's *The Tenant of Wildfell Hall* and George Eliot's *Middlemarch*, *Adam Bede* and *The Mill on the Floss* were the work of female authors, and were much concerned to explore the gradually changing role of women in the emerging bourgeois contexts of post-industrial England. Thus, while the heroines of such works have still to contend with the constraints of class and patriarchy that have traditionally conspired—in many if not most human cultures—to keep women in their very subservient place, such females are also clearly struggling towards a degree of liberation and independence from such pressures in a way that would have been unthinkable to such of their literary forebears as Iphigenia, Cassandra, Ophelia, Miranda and Cordelia. Thus, while Charlotte Bronte's Jane Eyre is clearly no less dependent for her security and reputation on the oppressive system of bourgeois patriarchy than her ancient Greek sisters, she refuses—even in prospect of loss of her romantic involvement with Rochester—to compromise the moral principles by which she clearly defines her identity and self-respect. In consequence, it is clearly by the standard of Jane's evident (if occasionally headstrong) moral virtues that the characters of most others in the novel are measured and found wanting.

On the other hand, a rather less flattering picture of the new English heroine is drawn in Jane Austen's *Emma*. While Emma is apparently beautiful (as Jane is not), intelligent and of independent spirit, she is also—perhaps lacking experience of the fires of adversity in which Jane's practical wisdom has been forged—somewhat spoiled and too full of herself. Like many others without proper occupation and with too much time on her hands, she is easily drawn to meddling in the affairs of others in the belief that she knows better than they what is good for them. In this regard, the narrative structure of the novel tracks the various embarrassing muddles and predicaments in which Jane becomes embroiled in the course of various attempts to manage and manipulate others. Still, the point of the novel is clearly to trace Emma's gradual appreciation—much under the critical influence of her eventual spouse George Knightly—of her moral and spiritual shortcomings. At all events, such close study of the moral development and progress of literary characters is clearly the staple fare of the nineteenth-century English novel. Thus, for example, Charles Dickens' *Great Expectations*—as Austen's *Emma*—traces the moral awakening through bitter experience of the central character 'Pip' (Philip) from the delusions and prejudices into which he has sunk by association with a particular privileged class and the typical schooling of that class.

On the other hand, William Makepeace Thackeray's Becky Sharp, the main protagonist of his *Vanity Fair*, presents a much more ambivalent portrait of a woman who — in a man's world — has had to embrace moral compromise in order to survive; though, as its title indicates, the novel is as much a critique of the society that has made Becky the way she is than it is of the anti-heroine herself. Generally, indeed, the nineteenth-century English novel is greatly preoccupied with the (often adverse) effects on character of various forms of social grooming and stereotyping and with the prospects of moral liberation from such constraints. And, though we cannot pause to explore the field more fully here, much other nineteenth-century fiction — abroad as well as closer to home — is no less concerned with character study. So, while many of the great nineteenth-century European and Russian novels are certainly also focused on large issues of revolution and social change, others — such as Flaubert's *Madame Bovary* and Tolstoy's *Anna Karenina* — are no less concerned with the effects on character, not least of women, of various modern societal developments and pressures. In the next chapter, however, we shall return — closer to the formative spirit of the Jubilee Knightly Virtues project — to some rather earlier literary explorations of character in moral action.

Chapter Four

The Knightly Virtues of Medieval Chivalry

The Story So Far

To recap briefly, we have considered two principal respects in which the narratives or stories of cultural inheritance and/or more recent creative and imaginative writing may serve to shape or form moral vision, character and conduct. First, the great myths and legends of religious and other cultural heritage explore the eternal themes of human freedom, purpose and destiny. Is there any real meaning in or purpose to human life? Is a worthwhile life a matter of unbridled freedom or of obedience to higher (moral or other) authority? Are human agents anyway able to determine their own destiny against the forces of nature, chance or fate? Secondly, much great literature from classical Greek drama and Shakespeare to modern drama and novel has been as much if not more concerned with study of the personal and social implications for human character of this or that moral value, perspective or course of action. What part do the characters of Oedipus or Orestes play in the tragic events in which they are caught up? What are the effects on the characters of Macbeth or Othello of their respective ambition and jealousy? What may be said for or against the ways in which Jane Eyre or Becky Sharpe cope with adversity? That said, many time-honoured and cherished human narratives and stories are clearly concerned with exploration of the inevitable interplay between the great themes of human purpose and destiny and individual character. While it is true that the main protagonists of the *Epic of Gilgamesh* or of the *Genesis* story of Adam and Eve serve largely symbolic, allegorical and archetypal functions in these narratives and so do not provide us with much character detail, and that Jane Austen's tale of Emma does not conspicuously address larger philosophical questions of the meaning of human life or the nature of free will, Euripides *Medea* and *Iphigenia*, Shakespeare's *Macbeth* and *Hamlet* and Dostoevsky's *Brothers Karamazov* and *Crime and Punishment* are evidently concerned to explore both the larger questions of human meaning and purpose *and* particular aspects of human character and agency — as well as, of course, something of the rich and complex interplay between these.

The Character of Medieval Chivalry

In this regard, one theme of imaginative literature that has proved to be of enduring human interest — in western culture, but also more widely — is that which concerns the quests for both worldly fame and honour *and* moral and spiritual progress of the noble kings and knights of medieval European chivalry. Such narratives — particularly those of the legendary (though more likely mythological) British King Arthur and his Knights of the Round Table — are likely to be familiar to modern readers and audiences from latter day pulp literary, cinematic and televised re-workings or adaptations of Sir Thomas Malory's fifteenth-century prose masterpiece *Morte D'Arthur* (1986) and Alfred Lord Tennyson's no less remarkable nineteenth-century poem *Idylls of the King* (1989). However, these tales were themselves drawn from earlier medieval ballads of Wolfram von Eschenbach, Chretienne de Troyes, Robert de Boron and others, celebrating the knightly (and amorous) exploits of such time-honoured heroes of chivalry as Parsifal (Percival), Tristram, Lancelot, Roland, Galahad and El Cid. And whilst one should clearly not mistake the highly embroidered and romanticised stories of chivalry and knighthood of the medieval troubadours and their later interpreters for an accurate history of the times in which they are purportedly set, it cannot be doubted that their enduring appeal—especially to young but also older readers and audiences—has much to do with a widely shared human psychological appreciation of the deeper moral and spiritual goals to which these great works of human imagination have managed to give extra-ordinary form and expression. From this viewpoint, the attraction of the young to contemporary popularized TV re-workings of stories of Arthur, Lancelot and Merlin may not be easily dismissed in terms of the primal appeal to young males of violent physical domination, or to young females of fairytale princess girl power, and evidently taps some deeper human vein of moral and spiritual striving or aspira-tion. Indeed, this seems to be keenly appreciated, as we shall shortly see, in a definitive attempt to debunk medieval ideas of knighthood and chivalry in one of the great classics of early modern fiction.

Wherein, then, lies the truth of medieval knighthood and chivalry? To begin with, we should be under no illusion that the eras or centuries of knightly derring-do of which the medieval troubadours and balladeers wrote were probably unspeakably bloody and brutal. (For a useful introduction to historical knights and chivalry, see Gies 1984.) To a large extent, it is likely that such times would have well fitted the description that Thomas Hobbes gave of pre-civil society as 'a war of all against all' in which life for many—not least the oppressed lower social orders of a rigidly hierarchical feudal society—would have been 'nasty, brutish and short' (Hobbes 1969, p. 186). Indeed, it is notable that while the knightly heroes of the troubadours, Malory and Tennyson lay claim to being champions of truth, faith and justice, this seems to be mostly a matter of rescuing noble ladies by slay-ing the evil knights into whose clutches they had fallen, and hardly at all about performing charitable works for the com-mon poor who hardly ever receive much if any mention in the classic literary annals of chivalry. Indeed, in most historical and other writings of the medieval period, those on the bottom rungs of the feudal system have the very lowest profile and their sufferings — and no doubt their economic and other exploitation by those above them — get little more than token mention. That said, it seems likely that life for many of those nobles and other feudal rulers who set themselves up as custodians or protectors of the common people — though doubtless more comfortable in albeit draughty castles — was also hardly less insecure or precarious. In feudal societies, in which might was right, it would be a constant struggle for those in power — often no doubt by dint of their own violent seizure of power or inheritance of such from others who had seized power before them — to secure it against continual threat of violent usurpation or invasion by rivals bent on acquiring more power. In this regard, medieval political authority would more often have resembled mafia mob rule and gang war than modern popular government. Insofar, medieval knighthood clearly had its source and origins in the brutal thuggery of local warlords who had little thought to anything much beyond their own personal advancement and advantage.

Given this, it is natural to ask how medieval knighthood came to be associated with — and even sometimes actually inspired by — loftier moral ideals of service to others, or at least something beyond the vainglorious self and/or its very local loyalties. And, to be sure, the short answer to this is that the higher authority to which local feudal rivalries were eventually expected or required to submit was — in western Europe — the universal church of Christ in Rome. In brief, while we may now see with the wisdom of historical (especially post-reformation) hindsight that the Church of the Holy Roman Empire was often no less power-seeking and corrupt than those over whom it sought to exercise some political and social control, it could lay claim to a spiritual and moral authority over the souls of men that at least aspired to something beyond naked self-interest. Moreover, insofar as the church preached and promoted an absolute morality of

Christian reciprocal justice and love as a necessary means to the salvation of the soul—and concomitant avoidance of post-mortal fires of hell—it could be expected to compel some submission and obedience from high and low alike. To an extraordinary extent the church was also able to impress or superimpose this ideal of general moral regard for others —irrespective of station—upon an already established warrior code of honour that laid down specific rules for martial combat and decent treatment of the vanquished. Precisely, this warrior code of respect for honourable foes, embellished or overlaid by a Christian vision of salvation as a matter of the cultivation of more egalitarian values and virtues of respect and fair treatment for all irrespective of station—with perhaps particular regard to the most vulnerable, such as the poor, the defenceless, the 'weaker' sex and children—developed eventually into the chivalric code of knightly conduct. On the back of this development, in addition to the warrior virtues of valour, loyalty and honour, knights would be encouraged to cultivate virtues of service (*noblesse oblige*), justice as universal respect and fairness, gallantry and graciousness (especially to the 'fair sex') and religious commitment. Indeed, as medieval Christendom and the frontiers of Europe came under threat and pressure from Muslim and other religious 'infidels' from the seventh century onwards, Christian knights were increasingly expected to include armed defence of the faith in the Holy Land or the Iberian peninsula among their knightly obligations and commitments.

So for better or worse, from the viewpoint of modern secular sensibility, there can be little doubt that the medieval romances of King Arthur, Parsifal (or Percival), Tristram, Lancelot and Roland are not just great human stories and narratives, they are more particularly *Christian* stories and narratives. It is therefore impossible to understand the personal ambitions, interpersonal relationships, political goals and moral and spiritual strivings of the characters of such narratives without some appreciation of their deep cultural roots in pre-modern Christian culture. In this regard, for example, in Sir Thomas Malory's ambitious but variably successful attempt to draw together the rather disparate narratives of the troubadours into something like a single coherent narrative, perhaps the most significant theme is that of the 'Grail' quest—in terms of which, as we shall see, the very characters and identities of central Arthurian characters are defined. Hence, to begin with, it needs to be appreciated that the quest for the Holy Grail—variously, if not downright ambiguously conceived as the cup of the Last Supper or the chalice in which the drops of Christ's blood were caught at His crucifixion—is symbolic of the ultimate Christian quest for moral and spiritual perfection, via cultivation not just of the cardinal virtues of wisdom, temperance and courage, but of the theological virtues of faith, hope and love (understood as universal charity or *caritas* and compassion). Further to this, the checkered relationships of the central Arthurian characters of Arthur, Guinevere and Lancelot can hardly be grasped apart from some appreciation of the tensions between the more worldly chivalric conception of courtly love and the Christian ideal of spiritual or divine love. But likewise, the famous Arthurian round table also evidently symbolizes the aspiration of a Christian king to forge a new political order of equal rights and participation that transcends the hierarchy and autocracy of the old feudal order, which—despite the paradox that the feudal order had itself been greatly authorized and upheld by church teaching of the divine right of kings—also anticipates, in Christian spirit and by virtue of Christian heritage, the egalitarian character and political institutions of modern post-enlightenment western liberal democracy.

Character in Medieval Chivalry:
King Arthur and His Knights

At all events, Sir Thomas Malory's fifteenth-century masterpiece *Morte D'Arthur*, is no doubt the definitive and most concentrated source of stories of the legendary British King

Arthur and his Knights of the Round Table—though, as mentioned, these narratives had medieval forerunners and have been constantly reworked and retold down the centuries to the present day. That said, Alfred Lord Tennyson's *Idylls of the King*, composed during a period of romantic nineteenth-century nostalgia for an alleged—and perhaps largely imagined—pre-industrial golden age of romance and chivalry, has also been an enduring and influential source of Arthurian themes, and modern fictional and cinematic re-workings of Arthurian legends have clearly drawn as often upon Tennyson as Malory. As also already noted, however, the extent to which the Round Table stories constitute a single unified narrative—given their diverse western European origins and sources—turns mainly on the interweaving of *three* main themes or motifs. First, there is what might be called the *mythic* or heroic narrative which focuses mainly upon the Tolkeinesque struggle of good to triumph over evil in an enchanted world of dragons, wizards, shape-shifting and magical swords in lakes and stones. Secondly, there is the religious or *spiritual* narrative of the quest for the Holy Grail, which is the ultimate redemptive goal of the human souls of Logres, Camelot and the Round Table. Thirdly, however, there is what we may call the human or *interpersonal* narrative, which concentrates more upon the vexed and more worldly relationships of King Arthur, Queen Guinevere and her lover, the 'first knight' Sir Lancelot—though such more shadowy figures as the sorcerer Merlin, the enchantress Morgan le Fay and Arthur's evil son and nephew Sir Mordred are also implicated in this particular drama.

Although what we have called the mythic aspect of the Arthurian legend is by no means devoid of real philosophical and psychological interest, not least to scholars operating at the rich interfaces of theology, anthropology and depth psychology, present interest in the Arthurian legends lies mainly in the moral and spiritual crises and tensions which arise in the spaces between the spiritual and interpersonal narratives. Insofar as the Holy Grail represents the ultimate moral and spiritual benchmark of Arthurian virtue and chivalry, the final 'horizon of significance' (see Taylor 1989) against which all human aspiration stands to be measured and judged, the quest for the Grail by the often less than perfect companions of the Round Table is a prime site of that eternal conflict between truth and inspiration which Santayana (1968, p. 219) regarded as the very essence of tragedy — and it is arguably the quest for the Grail, more than the machinations of Morgan and Mordred, which ultimately proves to be a bridge too far for the fellowship of Camelot. It is the Grail, then, that ultimately defines for good or ill the complex characters of Arthurian narrative. From this viewpoint, we may first observe that while he would normally be regarded as the main focus of the epic, King Arthur himself provides less than promising material for character study. Although portrayed as a noble and courageous man who is also prey to very human fits of anger, jealousy and lust, Arthur also largely inhabits the shadowy world of myth and is to that extent remote from the messy detail of human character. Indeed, in some re-workings of the story, it seems a problem for Guinevere that Arthur moves and has his being too far above the plane of ordinary flesh and blood humanity to be a proper object of female love. At this mythic level, Arthur seems to exist as a spiritual archetype who moves in a larger-than-life allegorical world of moonshine, magic and monsters: as the 'the hero with a thousand faces' (Campbell 1993) he represents the hazards, trials and tribulations of everyman and hence of no man in particular. At the more social and political level, however, the immortality of the once and future king might also be held to reside more in the liberal-democratic legacy of the Round Table than in the actual body of a sleeping patriarch awaiting in a rusting suit of armour some moment of supernatural physical resurrection. At this level, Arthur is (despite being actually Welsh, British or at least Celtic) the spirit of all freeborn Englishmen, wherever and whenever they struggle against the opposite and equal dangers of anarchy and tyranny.

Arthur himself is therefore both more than a character and less than a character—which may well explain the trouble that some versions of the legend seem to have had in offering a well-drawn human portrait of him. Beyond Arthur, however, the Arthurian romances are teeming with wildly colourful, vividly drawn and greatly contrasting characters: the effortless but driven confidence and superiority of Sir Lancelot; the lusty impetuosity of Sir Gawaine; the twisted malevolence of Sir Mordred; the patience and humility of Sir Gareth; the morbid despondency of Sir Geraint; the artless innocence and simplicity of Sir Percival; the earthy no-nonsense honesty of Sir Bors; the vindictive self-importance of Sir Kay; and so on. To these, of course, we should in any full consideration of Arthurian character add the many strong portrayals of good and bad female character: the tormented passion of Guinevere; the ambitious scheming of Vivien (or Morgan); the morbid amour of Elaine of Astolat; and so forth. For present purposes, however, we may here concentrate on the more knightly virtues of the male Arthurian characters.

Where, then, should one begin any examination of the virtues and vices of the *personis dramatae* of Arthurian legend? It is almost certain that any straw poll of the key players of the Round Table stories—after or along with Arthur, Guinevere and/or Merlin—would be likely to identify Sir Lancelot as the most central and compelling Arthurian character. On the face of it, Sir Lancelot is the very embodiment of the virtues of nobility, chivalry, justice and courage that characterize Arthurian knighthood: while he is absolutely unbeatable in battle, he is nevertheless second to none in his charity and generosity to those less well placed or favoured, and is invariably first to rise to the defence— usually in the face of the boorish bullying of the court seneschal Sir Kay—of those such as Sir Percival and Sir Gareth who pursue humbler routes into the Round Table fellowship. Sir Lancelot is universally admired by men and adored by women, and in Boorman's fine screen version of the legend (*Excalibur* 1981), the drunken Sir Gawaine exclaims that there is no one in the court who does not think him a god. However, it is significant that like Sir Gawaine — the knight who may come nearest to matching him in strength, nobility and courage—Sir Lancelot is explicitly denied that access to the Holy Grail that is granted to his son Sir Galahad, his nephew Sir Bors and his friend Sir Percival. As the ultimate horizon of Arthurian significance and benchmark of Round Table virtue, the Holy Grail is vouchsafed only to those who have shown themselves to be worthy, and Sir Lancelot—regarded in terms of worldly values and aspirations as the noblest of the Arthurian fellowship—is judged to be unworthy.

In this light, we might first look at the characters of the three knights Sir Galahad, Sir Percival and Sir Bors who actually succeed in their quest for the Holy Grail, and begin by asking whether and to what extent they conform to the Aristotelian ideal of good character as virtue explored in this work. In the first place, they certainly all conform to the general pattern of Aristotelian virtue as a state of the soul in which there is little or no conflict between reason, feeling and volition: while Sir Galahad, Sir Bors and Sir Percival experience the temptations of other men, their desires and inclinations are refined or cultivated to the extent that any dishonourable conduct is mostly unthinkable to them, and they do not therefore experience what Aristotle calls the *continent* agent's (albeit successful) struggle with emotional or motivational ambivalence. That said, insofar as the moral characters and qualities of the Grail knights are interestingly different, it might seem that they correspond to three rather *different* conceptions of virtue as distinguished in Aristotle's *Nicomachean Ethics*. A first distinction marked by Aristotle is between a general level of virtue to which human moral agents might reasonably be expected to aspire and that to which he refers as 'heroic' virtue—a more superhuman or 'godlike' level of attainment that is quite beyond the reach of human agents. However, it is precisely such god-like or divine virtue that seems to be possessed by Sir Galahad, the illegitimate son of Sir Lancelot and Elaine (though not, apparently, the Elaine of Astolat). Sir Galahad is the true soldier of Christ who dispatches his enemies only from necessity, never out of malice or vainglory, and his life is characterized by an uncompromising Platonic-Christian search for the ultimate vision of the good. In his unswerving imitation of Christ, Sir Galahad ultimately achieves the virtue of God as man in Christ, and so — with nothing more for a Christian soul to achieve — he is more or less assumed into heaven in a state of beatitude. Insofar, it would seem — by virtue of a distinctive Christian theology of 'godmanhood' — that Sir Galahad achieves a large measure of that very heroic virtue Aristotle reserves for divine rather than human agents.

Still, Aristotle also distinguishes non-heroic virtue from what he is inclined to call *natural* virtue. Natural virtue is for Aristotle a kind of unschooled or untutored goodness of the sort romantics have often linked to uncorrupted childhood innocence, and which seems to be significantly characteristic of the second most important Grail knight, Sir Percival. Indeed, though sometimes held to be of noble parentage, Percival arrives at Arthur's court under the wing of Sir Lancelot as very much as a child of nature reared in the wilderness, and he seems precisely to have the simple and innocent heart that eighteenth- and nineteenth-century romantics identified with Rousseauian natural or pre-social man. Although, like Sir Galahad, Sir Percival is touched with genuine holiness, the goodness he radiates is largely spontaneous and uncultivated, he acts from the basic impulses of a naturally open heart, and the undeniable reasonableness of his virtue seems nevertheless to lack the contemplative or visionary dimension of Sir Galahad's. However, the heroic virtue of Sir Galahad and the natural virtue of Sir Percival may both be contrasted with the character of Sir Bors who is perhaps the best exemplar of that capacity for sound and sensible deliberation—as well as good heartedness—that Aristotle refers to as *phronesis*, moral wisdom or sometimes simply prudence. In short, Sir Bors represents the genuine salt of the earth who do what is right as a matter of plain decency. Unlike Sir Galahad, Bors is practical more than contemplative, and he is also worldly wiser than Sir Percival, but he is nevertheless unfailingly honest, just, courageous and loyal—as well as entirely devoid of vanity or *hubris*. Moreover, unlike Sir Galahad and Sir Percival, Sir Bors is the only successful Grail knight to return to Arthur's court after the quest: whereas the saintly Sir Galahad is assumed into heaven, and the holy, innocent Sir Percival remains behind as the new guardian of the Grail in the castle of the Fisher King, it is the destiny of Sir Bors—as the Aristotelian man of civic virtue—to return to the court to put his wisdom and goodness to work in the larger practical and political affairs of men.

Still, the Grail knights are all in their different ways virtuous, and it is proof of their virtue that they are successful in their quest for the Grail. By the same token, however, those who do not achieve the Grail fail because they are less than virtuous—and this, among others, includes those such as Sir Lancelot and Sir Gawaine who are otherwise regarded as the greatest knights of the Round Table. Clearly, moreover, since the most conspicuous lack of success seems to be that of Sir Lancelot, it is worth asking why Arthur's first knight fails. The most obvious reason that might be suggested for Sir Lancelot's failure is that he harbours in his heart the sin of an adulterous love for Arthur's queen Guinevere. But it is actually not clear why such love—which in a sense he cannot help—should actually disqualify him from the virtuous condition of more successful Grail aspirants. To be sure, the problem here may seem conceptual, and to be related to Aristotle's important distinction between continent and virtuous agents—according to which the so-called continent, while able to achieve moral ends of virtue, nevertheless fall short of full virtue because their desires, emotions and appetites are still at odds with such ends. The trouble with continent agents, on this view, is that they are still moved by desires that the virtuous agent has outgrown or transcended. That said, it should be noted that this is not the simple distinction between those who are tempted and resist, and those who are not at all tempted. After all, if agents are never humanly tempted, they could hardly be described as virtuous either. So what could be the difference between Sir Lancelot, whose adulterous desire for Guinevere is in some versions of the narrative quite unconsummated — precisely because the knight regards such adulterous desire as dishonourable — and the virtuous who would also dismiss such desire on the same grounds?

It is arguable that the key to Sir Lancelot's failure to achieve the full virtue of the successful Grail aspirant is revealed in a brief episode — related by Malory (1986, book XV, chapters v and vi) — of his own Grail quest. In the course of his unsuccessful mission, Sir Lancelot stumbles across a conflict between two bands of knights, one group clad entirely in white, the other in black. Since the black knights are clearly being bested by the white knights, Sir Lancelot — following his general inclination to side with the underdog (though also apparently without hesitating to enquire about the bone of contention) — pitches in on the side of the black knights. After doing his utmost, however, the greatest knight of the Round Table is driven from the field by the white knights, and then falls into ever greater despair and despondency — holding himself, by virtue of his unprecedented defeat, to be a greater sinner than ever. Shortly after, however, he meets a holy woman who explains to him that whereas the black knights — to whose aid he had rushed — stood for worldly honour and aspiration, the white knights who defeated him were (perhaps a vision of) the truly virtuous of God's elect. Sir Lancelot's support for the black knights appears (perhaps with Freudian interpretation) to have symbolized his attachment to reputation and vainglory, and his general spiritual and moral unfitness for the company of the fully virtuous. On this view, Sir Lancelot's basic problem stems from his chronic and driven over-achievement: as one who has to be the best at everything, he is also unable to live with the thought of the ultimate humiliation (for him) of failure. The Grail, on the other hand, is the ultimate symbol of humiliation, of the God who is able to face the final test of self-doubt and worldly rejection on the cross.

It is also arguably Sir Lancelot's deep-seated pride or vainglory that explains what is really wrong with his hopeless attachment to Guinevere. The trouble is that for the ultimate overachiever, there could hardly be any other worthy object of his love than the highest and most beautiful woman in the land, who is also — more or less inevitably — the wife of his best friend the king. But, of course, the object of his love is also thereby neither realistically nor honourably attainable. In this regard, there is again a certain perverse vanity about Sir Lancelot's unswerving and mostly chaste devotion to Guinevere that relieves him of the unromantic burdens — as well as the risk of failure — of love for any real woman (such as, for example, Elaine, the mother of his own son). Sir Lancelot can always therefore avoid the risk of human failure, and any consequent threat to his self-esteem, by vanquishing the men and renouncing the women — albeit in the name of worthy ideals of honour and chivalry. Hence, while Sir Lancelot is largely a species of Aristotle's continent agent — his motives and conduct are characterized by utter disciplined commitment to honourable ideals — he also seems driven to honour for the sake of honour, rather than to honour as a means to higher self-transcendent goods or goals. As the tragic victim of his own success, he is unable to free himself from the corrosive *hubris* and vanity that is, in albeit different ways, quite absent from the conduct of Sir Galahad, Sir Percival and Sir Bors.

Moreover, while many Arthurian heroes are — more or less by definition — individuals of strong will and disciplined character, most would seem to be continent agents like Sir

Lancelot rather than men of virtue like the three Grail knights. This may well be true even of those who are—like Sir Lancelot—possessed of the almost complete self-control that may seem at first sight indistinguishable from virtue. Another complex and conflicted knight who found his way to the Round Table—apparently from the Welsh *Mabinogion* via Chretienne de Troyes—is the hero of a story in both Malory and Tennyson of Geraint and Enid. On a mission to defend the honour of Queen Guinevere against those who have slighted her, Geraint—one of the noblest champions of Arthur's court—encounters and falls in love with the beautiful and virtuous Enid whom he subsequently marries. However, having formerly been one of the great Round Table overachievers, Geraint becomes so besotted with Enid that he can no longer tear himself away from her to attend to his knightly and chivalric duties—which soon gives rise to court murmurings, behind his back, that he is no longer the man he was. While Geraint remains oblivious to the gossip, Enid overhears it and is wracked with guilt at the thought that she is responsible for her spouse's diminished reputation. One night, Geraint overhears a sobbing and half-awake Enid murmur that she is no longer worthy of Geraint. The besotted Geraint interprets this to mean that Enid has betrayed him with another man and in consequence drags her off on a quest that seems partly designed to mete out cruel and humiliating punishment to Enid and partly to regain his bruised self-esteem. In the event, this escapade—in which Geraint meets and defeats a seemingly endless succession of opponents—turns out to be a journey of moral and spiritual self-discovery in which he is forced to grow up via dawning appreciation of what both genuine honour and love actually mean. Rather like Lancelot, Geraint seems to have somewhat immature romantic notions of honour, courage and love, from which he is easily distracted and which are readily undermined by insecurity, jealousy and lack of trust. In this regard, Geraint—again like Lancelot—seems merely continent rather than fully virtuous, and needs to learn by bitter experience what honour and love really mean before he can make progress to genuine virtue. Incidentally, the Geraint and Enid story is also a good example of a narrative genre in which a rather confused and immature man is redeemed by the love and constancy of a more mature and virtuous woman. At all events, while the Grail knights Sir Galahad, Sir Percival and Sir Bors all appear well endowed with such moral and spiritual virtues as faith, trust and (other-regarding) love, it seems that such virtues are above all manifest — somewhat paradoxically — in their not being pursued by them *as* virtues. In short, the main pitfall of the pursuit of virtuous goals by the continent may not be that they are not successfully pursued, but that they are not pursued as the virtuous should pursue them.

At all events, while there are Arthurian heroes who — despite their flaws — appear continent, at least to the extent of exercising iron self-control in the pursuit of generally honourable or laudable goals, many more seem more complex human mixtures of continence and incontinence insofar as they are self-controlled in some respects, but clearly vulnerable to temptation in others. In this connection, another leading light of Arthur's court who fails the Grail quest is Sir Gawaine. While Sir Gawaine is the hero of many Arthurian adventures, second only to Sir Lancelot in knightly nobility, honour and courage — and the steadfast friend of Sir Lancelot until the accidental slaying by the latter of Gawaine's brothers Sir Gareth and Sir Gaheris — he is also turned back from his quest for the Grail for a range of very worldly shortcomings. On the face of it, Sir Gawaine's *akrasia* or incontinence would appear to be of both the key Aristotelian varieties of intemperance and impetuosity. On the one hand, he is sometimes held to be especially vulnerable to the more temporal attachments of self-love and sensual pleasure: in his greatest adventure with the Green Knight, he avoids disgracing himself with his host's wife only by a hair's breadth, and the entire narrative is one of moral compromise in which honour and courage are barely equal to vanity and self-preservation (Burrow 1972). On the other, despite his efforts to give fair hearing to both sides of a case, he is also not slow to take offence or bear a grudge — and it is largely such impetuosity that leads to his ultimate tragic conflict with his former friend Sir Lancelot. In this respect, much of the attraction of Sir Gawaine may be that unlike the Grail knights he is precisely that complex and very human mixture of strength and weakness, success and failure, to which most of us can readily relate from our own experience.

Reading *Morte D'Arthur* or *Idylls of the King* in the light of the baser failings of character that Aristotle identifies in the *Nicomachean Ethics*, however, it is clear that as well as virtuous and good — but sometimes intemperate — Arthurian heroes, there are utterly weak, vicious and villainous knights, and these would appear to range from the almost totally incontinent or *akratic* — those who fail to live up to or who betray the knightly ideals, though in some sense or at some level they nevertheless appreciate the value and justice of such ideals — to those who would appear to reject such ideals from motives of avarice, self-interest, power-seeking or just plain malice. Of the many power-hungry kings and princes who initially oppose King Arthur's accession, and those knights who seem constantly bent on the apparently more libidinously driven practice of incarcerating fair damsels in castles, many if not most come to see the error of their ways as a result of judicious unhorsing by Arthur's lieutenants. At the more unrepentant end of the scale, however, Sir Mordred and Sir Agravaine seem to be in the grip of more sinister goals and desires. Sir Agravaine, to be sure, seems to be little more than a weak vassal of Mordred who has been totally suborned or corrupted to the service of his brother — a prime example of the easily led who have little real will of their own. The twisted and malevolent Sir Mordred, on the other hand, typifies those who, in their embrace of evil and destruction almost for its own sake, are more vicious or *akolastic* than *akratic* in Aristotle's terms.

Indeed, Sir Mordred seems the kind of agent of whom we might ask whether he is mad or bad — recognizing that any answer to this question is likely to be more a label for, than a solution to, the problem. At one level, Sir Mordred seems driven by a perfectly intelligible if unenviable hunger for power. At another, however, it appears that unlike Sir Galahad — another illegitimate son of a guilt-ridden and absent father — Sir Mordred takes sadistic pleasure in cruelty towards and humiliation of others. His unfortunate parentage and his father's rejection of him go some way towards explaining his anger and bitterness; but they cannot entirely excuse or justify his dark self-absorption and his will to absolute destruction of all that is good.

To be sure, the question of whether Sir Mordred is mad or bad need not be an entirely idle one: at one level, it is a perfectly reasonable question about the extent of his moral or criminal responsibility for his actions. If something goes snap in Sir Mordred's brain whenever he embarks on a murderous rampage, then he has no rational control over his actions and we may well feel compelled to commit him as a suitable case for treatment rather than sentence him to a term of community service. However, it may also be a mistake to assume that any distinction between madness and badness is primarily or exclusively expressible in scientific or statistical rather than normative terms: that, as it were, the categories of madness and moral responsibility are mutually exclusive. From this viewpoint, it may be that madness has often no less a spiritual as a pathological cause or dimension than badness, and that we can become mad as much by the choices we make or by the values by which we have chosen to live as by the influence on us of the genetic or environmental cards we have been dealt (see Jacobs 2001). Indeed, it is clear that many perfectly healthy individuals of good education and fortunate background have been driven to what many would regard as insane extremes of criminal conduct by fanatical commitment to ideals operating more as triggers for the release of self-focused rancour or resentment than as incentives to the greater good in whose name such crime is committed.

In this connection, indeed, the question of whether Sir Mordred is mad or bad may be formally analogous to the rather more theological issue of whether the virtue of a Sir Galahad, Sir Percival or Sir Bors is a matter of grace or works. On the face of it, it may seem providentially unfair that whereas Sir Lancelot and Sir Gareth have to struggle for purity or humility, it seems to come so easily — as a matter of divine favour or natural endowment — to the Grail knights. But just as it may be a mistake to think that we can never have responsibility for our ultimate moral alienation, autism or derangement, or that such derangement always absolves us of responsibility, so it seems a mistake to suppose that the temperamental or other gifts we have received are such as to render any and all effort redundant. Sir Lancelot is certainly no Sir Galahad: but we have no reason to suppose either that with different choices he might not have attained the virtues of his son, or that those virtues could have been attained without any effort on his offspring's part. The importance of Aristotle's classic discussion of the internal relationship between character and voluntary agency is that it shows the considerable extent to which both vice and virtue are consequences, not so much of what happens to people, but of how they use the natural and other talents and benefits they have been vouchsafed. In this respect, we should bear in mind that although both Sir Galahad and Sir Mordred were the illegitimate sons of fathers who abandoned them, the former went on to be the holiest of saints whereas the latter proceeded to be the blackest of sinners. At all events, it is arguable that the rich and colourful array of Aristotelian character types who enliven the pages of the Arthurian romances provide as good explorations as we could possibly wish for of the general structure of moral and spiritual growth, and of the various trials to which such human aspiration is heir.

The Educative Potential
of Knights Past and Present

So, while it probably hardly needs saying that the young people who are evidently still widely drawn to the Arthurian myths and legend — to the evergreen stories of Arthur, Guinevere, Merlin, Lancelot, Tristram and others — are not primarily so drawn for their moral educational potential, it is no less clear such narratives may yet be aptly regarded as rich sources of insight into moral, spiritual and other human life and association. Indeed, it seems likely that such narratives have often served a significant educational function — not least in pre-literate societies — in assisting appreciation by the young of the ethical complexities of agency, character and motive, and of the way in which much if not most interpersonal association is implicated in the larger moral struggle of good against evil, or virtue against vice. In this regard, the colourful and variously heroic characters of such great human narratives as the Arthur and Grail legends have evidently been exhibited as objects of moral attraction and repulsion: whereas the characteristics of invariably triumphing heroes or heroines provide models to be imitated, those of knaves and villains are offered primarily as a warning — usually reinforced by the inevitably bad ends of those given to knavery — of the dire human consequences of vice. That said, this is not at all to exalt or approve of some of the moral ideals or values clearly presupposed to such narratives, or — yet more problematically — to ignore the likelihood that the more morally questionable aspects of such stories may often be those to which the young are or have been especially attracted. However glamorous the knights in their gaudy heraldic colours may appear, it should not be forgotten that real feudal knights and the medieval times in which they flourished were probably for the most part deeply authoritarian, brutal and unjust and that those on the butt end of feudal society may have had little enough to thank their overlords for. Indeed, the romantic warrior ideals and aspirations to so-called

honour, courage, unswerving loyalty and so on that motivated medieval knights may not have been too far removed
from the post-Nietzschean *ubermenschen* ideals of Hitler and
the Third Reich or from those of Emperor Hirohito's cruelly
feudal Knights of Bushido—and, indeed, it should not be
forgotten that the medieval legends of Parsifal and Tristan,
immortalized in the music of Wagner, actually served as
potent inspiration for Nazi madness.

In this light, it needs to be re-emphasized that the
Arthurian and grail narratives were highly romanticized and
morally idealized stories in terms of which a temporal but
also spiritual power—the Holy Roman Church—sought precisely to re-shape the often brutal regimes of medieval feudal
warlords according to Christian virtues and values. That
said, such re-shaping would have lasting influence in a very
inspiring picture or vision of knighthood as a beacon of
virtues of honour, courage and service—and in various
western European institutions and practices of titled public
recognition for such merit and service that have continued
down to the present day. To be sure, contemporary knights
and dames live in a very different world from that of medieval feudal society and seldom—except perhaps in the weird
and wonderful garb of titled pop and movie stars—appear
quite so glamorous. Indeed, all too many knighthoods and
other honours may seem nowadays conferred on those—
such as the creators and popularizers of vulgar art and artless music, those city financiers who seem to have made pots
of money at public expense and those perhaps more single-
mindedly bent on pursuing sporting fixations for purposes
of personal ambition—who might hardly be regarded as
models of public service. On top of this, there have been not
a few recent embarrassing exposures of titled figures of
media and commerce for a range of financial, sexual and
other crimes and irregularities that would disgrace the least
morally ambitious members of the local pub darts club. That
said, the constituency of contemporary knighthood is also
still graced by a range of distinguished academic, political,

philanthropic and other contributors to the common good who can clearly claim to have contributed to human service in the tradition of chivalric service romantically depicted by the likes of Malory and Tennyson—and perhaps actually exemplified by some knights of medieval yore. It is anyway in the general spirit of this knightly tradition, but also mindful that today's youngsters are more likely to be drawn imaginatively to King Arthur and Lancelot than to the modern knights of science, industry or commerce, that—in response to a Templeton invitation to explore the educational potential of the character virtues of knighthood and nobility—the Birmingham University Jubilee Centre for the Study of Character and Values launched its 2012 'Knightly Virtues' project focusing on bygone stories of chivalry, courage and honour, with a view to primary school exploration of some of the values and character virtues exemplified in such narratives. We shall therefore next take a closer look at the main stories on which this project chose to concentrate.

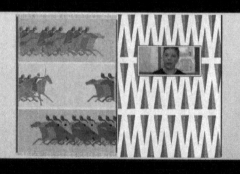

Chapter Five

The Stories
of the Knightly
Virtues Project

Selecting the Stories

To begin with, something needs to be said about the problems of story selection faced by the authors of the 'Knightly Virtues' project. Most of these problems turned on the awkward fact that despite the obvious attraction of past heroic narratives for people of various ages, social classes and genders, there is no avoiding that the stories are from an age in which the leading characters were — by definition — of one (ruling) class, one gender and for the most part one race and colour: in short, the noble knights of old were mainly upper-class white males. To be sure, the knightly heroes of King Arthur and other medieval romances do include some individuals of non-Caucasian race and colour (usually of Moorish origin), and there are others (such as Percival) who are at least alleged to have been humbly raised (though usually also unaware of noble origins). We should also not forget — as already indicated in the story of Geraint and Enid — that there are many heroines to be found in the Arthurian legends by contrast with whose conspicuous nobility, grace and wisdom, the defects of their male counterparts are all too evident. But it can still be hardly denied that lower social classes and other races are significantly underrepresented in Arthurian and other tales of medieval chivalry and that the role of women in an essentially pre-modern patriarchal society — however virtuous or noble — was for the most part a mostly passive and subservient one. In the event, this gave rise to two rather conflicting desires or inclinations in the planning of this project: on the one hand, in the main spirit of the discussion so far, there was a desire to reclaim some of the justly celebrated and nowadays neglected narratives of knighthood and chivalry for contemporary classroom consumption; on the other, there was a reluctance to focus on narratives that clearly excluded other than white male actors from the moral limelight. Thus, at some risk of compromising the initial rather more coherent but more exclusive focus on knightly heroes as such, it was eventually decided to add Shakespeare's *The Merchant of Venice* — featuring at centre stage a noble, wise and virtuous heroine — to the initially proposed stories of Gareth and Lynette, El Cid and Don Quixote. At all events, it was thought that adding Shakespeare to Cervantes and Marlow/Tennyson would also provide further exposure to some of the all-time greatest literary fare — educationally defensible by any standards — for participants in this project. However, it was also agreed that the story of the great contemporary black heroine Rosa Parks might be scheduled for exploration — along with other more culturally, racially or gender diverse figures — in later developments of the project.

Gareth and Lynette
(Sir Thomas Malory and Alfred Lord Tennyson)

Still, given that the initial main inspiration of the 'Knightly Virtues' project was to explore moral virtues of knighthood and chivalry, it seemed appropriate to draw the first narrative for classroom exploration from the stories of King Arthur and his Knights of the Round Table. In principle, there were many possible stories to choose, since many of the Arthurian legends — perhaps not least those involving the heroic and spiritual quest for the Holy Grail — evidently feature knights embarked on perilous quests that call for a range of virtuous qualities of character such as courage, fidelity and honesty. In the event, however, though not much connected with the Grail narrative, the Arthurian story of Gareth and Lynette seemed to fit the desired moral educational bill as well as, if not better than, any others. This story, which features prominently in both Malory's *Morte D'Arthur* and Tennyson's *Idylls of the King* concerns the youngest son of the King and Queen of Orkney, the brother of Gawaine, Gaheris, Agravaine and half-brother of Mordred. As the last of the brothers to leave the family home, his mother is reluctant to see him go too as well as anxious to keep him for as long as possible out of harm's way. To this end, she makes him promise to go *incognito* to the court of Arthur and work there as a kitchen boy for a year before undertaking any perilous quest. Dutifully so promising, Gareth goes to Camelot and asks King Arthur that he may be granted a request after a year's service as a kitchen boy. During this service, while Garth is very kindly treated by Sir Lancelot who seems to suspect his noble origins, he has to undergo much abuse and ill treatment at the hands of the curmudgeonly court steward Sir Kay who contemptuously dubs him 'Beaumains' or 'fair hands'. On completion of his year of kitchen drudgery, however, he is in a position to petition King Arthur to grant his own request for chivalrous employment. Thus, when—at this well-timed moment—a young noblewoman named Lynette comes to the court to plead for a knightly champion to help free her sister from the Red Knight by whom she is held against her will, Gareth's request to undertake this mission is granted by King Arthur.

At the outset of his quest, Gareth is pursued by an irate Sir Kay, incensed by Arthur's assignment of this noble mission to a kitchen boy. Kay challenges Gareth to a fight but is soon ignominiously unhorsed by Gareth. This contest is witnessed by Sir Lancelot, who—impressed by Gareth's evident courage and prowess—persuades him to disclose his hitherto concealed noble identity and status. However, the Lady Lynette, who has already received the appointment of a kitchen hand as her sister's champion to be an insult and humiliation—not least since she hoped that no less than Sir Lancelot himself might have taken up the challenge—dismisses Gareth's defeat of Kay as a fluke of luck and directs a barrage of insult and abuse at the young knight. This barrage is vigorously maintained throughout a series of increasingly violent encounters with a number of armed adversaries—at various fords en route—who all claim to be kin to the Red Knight. While Gareth has no trouble overcoming these opponents, Lynette appears not in the least impressed by Gareth's bravery and skill, and continues to pour scorn on the young knight—who nevertheless bears this with utmost dignity, patience, humility, courtesy and forbearance. It is only at the last stage of the quest when Gareth and Lynette finally reach the castle of the Red Knight—and Gareth prepares to meet an opponent with the very appearance of Death himself—that Lynette shows genuine signs of concern, sympathy and compassion for Gareth and tries to dissuade him from an encounter that she is convinced can lead only to his untimely demise. However, Gareth insists that he can only honourably complete a mission that he has sworn to undertake and rides forth to engage what he takes to be the last and most formidable of his opponents. In the event, Gareth unseats his adversary easily and his opponent turns out to be a young boy who has been left in the rear to guard the castle and the imprisoned Lyonesse while the real Red Knight and his brothers defended the fords along the way. In fact, Gareth had already defeated the Red knight in a previous encounter and sent him back as prisoner to Arthur's court. Thus, Gareth—whose courage, chivalry and patience are finally and fully appreciated by the repentant Lady Lynette—is able to free the captive Lady Lyonesse who he escorts back to Camelot as his betrothed. Lancelot reveals Gareth's true identity to Arthur and he is welcomed to the court of Camelot as one of the foremost champions of the Round Table.

While all the great Arthurian and Grail stories serve as wonderful vehicles for illustration and exploration of fundamental human values and virtues, the story of Gareth and Lynette highlights some beyond the usual knightly fare of honour, courage and martial prowess. To be sure, while Gareth is generally honourable, there is clearly one particular dimension or aspect of the larger package of knightly honour that stands out above others in this Arthurian narrative and which seems to be possessed by this young knight in abundance. This is something very like the virtue of humility. Thus, first, while Gareth is of noble — even royal — blood, he is clearly not at all inclined to capitalize on this advantage. While he could have gone to King Arthur's court claiming entitlement to membership of the Round Table by right of birth, Gareth goes *incognito* as a humble kitchen hand — clearly of a mind that no one is proved worthy of respect by virtue of social standing alone. For Gareth, the moral or other worth of any human agent requires to be proved by deeds and actions and such deeds are of value for what they are in themselves apart from their association with status or privilege. However, the other key dimension of Gareth's honour — the main focus of this Arthurian story — shows up in his remarkable patience and forbearance regarding the taunts, insult and humiliation of the Lady Lynette. Although Lynette's treatment of Gareth is as prejudiced, high-handed and graceless as it is possible to imagine, the young knight continues to bear this with the utmost courtesy, patience and restraint. Whereas the average reader cannot help thinking that he or she could not have resisted the urge to put Lynette firmly in her place — at least by the middle of the story — Gareth is the very soul of long-suffering patience and forbearance.

Humility is also, to be sure, a virtue of considerable interest in this particular story as well as in general. For one thing, from a certain influential philosophical perspective, it may seem problematic to regard humility as a universal virtue. Thus, according to the contemporary moral and social philosopher Alasdair MacIntyre (1981), whose defence of the moral educational value of literature and the arts we noticed and applauded earlier, what counts in any context as a virtue depends to a large extent on its place and status within a particular evolved or evolving cultural tradition, and—since moral traditions have evolved differently in response to diverse social and economic arrangements and practices in different places—we might or should expect 'rival' moral traditions to have emerged giving pride of place to different, even contradictorily opposed virtues. Indeed, one virtue that might be held to have variable cultural and moral status in this regard is that of humility. Thus, while humility is supposed to have gained moral importance and prominence with the western moral, religious and cultural rise and spread of Christianity, it is held not to have been a moral virtue in older pre-Christian warrior societies—such as that of pagan Homeric Greece—in which humility would not have been considered a (certainly 'manly') virtue and might even have been regarded as a vice. That said, one obvious difficulty with this perspective is that if humility in particular, or virtues in general, are held to be relative to specific social context in this way, how might they really count or qualify as genuine moral qualities at all? How could we reasonably esteem the self-restraint, patience and forbearance of Gareth in his dealings with Lynette as a virtue in the context of this Arthurian story, yet deny that it is or was a virtue in other contexts? If it is morally right to be patient and forbearing with this trying person or circumstance in this context, must it not *always* be right to be so?

What MacIntyre and moral and social theorists of such 'social constructivist' persuasion would probably say about Gareth's humility is that it precisely illustrates the 'rival traditions' thesis of the gradual social evolution of human moral concepts. On this essentially neo-idealist (basically Hegelian) perspective, it might appear that the Gareth's story illustrates perfectly how the historical emergence of a new moral perspective of medieval chivalry from two preceding rival and conflicting moral traditions—those of a heroic warrior society and Christianity—required some accommodating or compromising resolution of the moral tension between these views. In this case, indeed, it seems hard to deny some truth in this: we have already observed that the very idea of chivalry was essentially an attempt by the Christian church to impose some kind of moral restraint on the mafia-style conduct of feudal robber barons. However, to put matters thus is not so much to register the mutual accommodation of two independent and equally valid moral traditions, as to recognize the evident moral superiority of one tradition over another. The fact is that the pre-chivalric feudal barons had for the most part been an ignoble example of vicious and unprincipled arrogance, piracy and rapine—who, beyond a respect for brute force and the right of might, had been scarcely touched by any of the key moral values and virtues of honesty, justice and other-regard. From this viewpoint, there is surely a danger of moving—in the manner of socially and historically constructed conceptions of moral virtue of MacIntyrean variety—from the observation that some society did not *consider* humility (or whatever) to be a virtue to the conclusion that humility was not or could never have *been* a virtue in any such context. To be sure, this precisely parallels the epistemic error of concluding from the observation that past social constituencies believed the world to be flat that they had a different *knowledge* of earthly dimensions from that we have today.

Indeed, it is here worth noting that Aristotle—who died well before the advent of Christianity and who was probably culturally much closer to the heroic society—does seem to have rated due humility as a virtue, even though his conception of this is perhaps not quite a Christian one. Of course, insofar as Aristotle tended to be somewhat dismissive of such gentler social virtues as gratitude, as being too much beholden to others, his view of humility is also more self- than other-regarding. From this viewpoint, it is right to exhibit due humility not so much out of patient regard or forbearance for others, but in order to avoid the vicious extremes of abject self-abasement and unseemly pride or vanity (Aristotle 1941a, book 2, section 7). In this light, to be sure, he might have been more inclined to advise slapping Lynette about a bit to teach her proper manners, and perhaps less sympathetic to Gareth's patient endurance of her abusive onslaughts. All the same, we may recognize some family resemblance between Aristotelian self-regarding and Christian other-regarding humility in a shared concern with avoiding excess pride or vanity, over-focus on oneself and/or exaggeration of one's achievements. Both Christian and Aristotelian humility are concerned with arriving at a basically honest and balanced view of ourselves in relation to God or others that is as far as possible free from what Jean-Jacques Rousseau (1973) called *'amour propre'* or what existentialist philosophers have termed *'mauvais foi'*. This seems very much — with the added ingredients of patience and forbearance — what Gareth successfully shows towards Lynette and others in the Arthurian romance.

El Cid (Historical Legend)

Unlike Sir Gareth of Arthurian legend, El Cid (an Arab term meaning 'the Lord') was a real-life eleventh-century knight of minor Spanish nobility, named Rodrigo Diaz, who was born in the Castilian town of Vivar in 1043 and died in 1099 in Valencia. (For a recent history of El Cid, see Fletcher 1989.) Still regarded to this day as one of the greatest chivalric heroes of Spanish history, El Cid — like so many other revered historical figures — is as much the stuff of legend as of firm historical fact. However, the historical records testify fairly accurately to Rodrigo's extraordinary ability as a military commander, and to his courage, sense of honour and fairness as a man, in one of the most turbulent times of Spanish history, in which much of Spain was ruled by invading Muslim Moors (Arabs from North Africa). That said, the forces of Christianity and Islam were by no means severally united at this time and the political divisions, power struggles and intrigues of the day were as often *between* Christian and Christian or Muslim and Muslim as between Christian and Muslim—and much of Rodrigo's political and military career was to be spent in negotiation of these complexities. Indeed, as a young nobleman first at the court of Ferdinand the Great, King of Castille, and then in the service of his son and successor King Sancho, Rodrigo cut his military teeth—and won his spurs—in successful campaigns against both Moors and various Christian relatives of Ferdinard and Sancho who had periodic designs on the throne.

One of the celebrated episodes in the story of El Cid—to which a creditable modern cinematic version of the legend (Mann 1961) gives especial romantic attention—concerns Rodrigo's vexed relationship with his wife-to-be Ximena following his unfortunate slaying of her father, the king's champion Don Gomez. According to the story, Rodrigo's aged father, Diego Laynez, was insulted in public by Don Gomez who struck him in the face, and—being too old to respond to this slight by the mortal combat that knightly honour required—Diego was overcome by shame and despondency. Learning of this, the young Rodrigo—who was in some versions of the narrative already enamoured with or betrothed to Ximena—sought out Don Gomez to demand an apology from the champion. When Don Gomez refused to apologize, Rodrigo challenged him to combat in the heat of which the king's champion was slain. However, just as Rodrigo had felt committed to avenging the dishonour that had been visited on his father by Don Gomez, Ximena—who was bound by love for her father as well as loving Rodrigo—felt no less obligated by the honour codes of the times to avenge her father by attempts on the life of Rodrigo, a project that she seems to have pursued with some passion over a fairly long period. Although true love appears to have triumphed at length and Ximena was eventually fully reconciled with Rodrigo as wife and ever after devoted companion, Don Gomez's daughter presents a paradigm case of an agent caught not only between conflicting moral imperatives — in this case the demands of filial pity (if not of actual revenge) on the one hand and forgiveness on the other — but also between simultaneous emotions of love and anger (if not actual hate) for one and the same person.

At all events, moving on from the strong sense of honour that prompted him to avenge his father, another morally significant side of Rodrigo's character seems revealed by events — following hard on the heels of his killing of Don Gomez — when King Ferdinand appears to have banished the young knight from the court of Castile on account of his rather high-handed manner. Accompanied by a large retinue of loyal knightly admirers, Rodrigo left the court of Ferdinand and became soon embroiled in combat with the united forces of several Moorish kings bent on invading Castile. Rodrigo and his men soon put these armies to rout and in the process took five of their kings or nobles prisoner. While it appears to have been the usual expectation of the Christian royal authorities in whose name Rodrigo was defending Castile that he should put the leaders of these invading infidels to death, he seems to have mercifully spared and released them when they pledged not to renew any invasion of Castile. It seems to have been at this point that Rodrigo acquired the name 'El Cid' (Arabic for 'the Lord') — precisely bestowed on him by the vanquished Moorish kings. Moreover, before taking leave of El Cid, several of the kings swore firm allegiance to and friendship with him and it seems that from this point on Rodrigo was able to rely in his various campaigns on 'cross-cultural' support from Muslims as well as Christians. Clearly, however, the point of the story is that while Rodrigo was certainly hot in defence of personal and family honour, he was also merciful and also seems — perhaps even more at odds with the temper of the times — to have been committed to peace, tolerance and reconciliation with others as moral and political ideals. Still, as soon as King Ferdinand had wind of Rodrigo's victories against the Moors he was welcomed back to the court — though many courtiers were also jealous of his fame and sought ways to undermine him.

The narratives of El Cid also draw attention to other more spiritual qualities of the hero. When Rodrigo returned to the court of Castile and was reconciled and married to Ximena, the happy couple was allegedly given several Spanish cities as wedding presents by King Ferdinand. However, before embarking on new military campaigns in defence of Castile, Rodrigo recalled making a vow to undertake a pilgrimage to Santiago de Compostella, the shrine of the patron saint of Spain. On his way there, he is said to have distributed alms (charity) to the poor, and paused to recite prayers at every church and wayside shrine. His courtesy, gentleness and generosity to everyone he encountered on the pilgrimage was exemplary and legend has it that on one occasion he looked after a poor leper at a wayside inn, actually sharing his meal with the diseased outcast. In the middle of the night (so the story goes), Rodrigo awoke to find the leper gone, and — in his place — St Lazarus is said to have appeared, praising Rodrigo's charity and promising him worldly success and heavenly reward. Rodrigo concluded his pilgrimage with many further acts of piety, including the donation of a large sum of money for the establishment of a leper-house, which — in honour of the saint who appeared to him — was named 'St Lazarus'. At all events, the El Cid narrative is at pains to emphasize that Rodrigo's martial virtues of honour, courage and mercy, and his civic virtues of respect, tolerance and justice, were also augmented or perfected by such Christian spiritual and theological virtues as faith, hope and charity.

Following his pilgrimage, Rodrigo resumed his military campaigns in the service of King Ferdinand and the defence of Castile. In one notable episode of these campaigns Rodrigo was chosen to do battle as the king's champion in a territorial dispute between Don Ramiro of Aragon and King Ferdinand of Castile over Calahorra, a border town between

Aragon and Castile. Although Martin Gonzalez, the champion appointed by Don Ramiro, was a tried and tested knight of considerably greater combat experience than Rodrigo, the latter nevertheless succeeded in overcoming his opponent, securing Calahorra for Castile. Still, while this victory significantly enhanced the reputation of Rodrigo, and greatly reinforced the trust and favour he enjoyed in the opinion of King Ferdinand, it also further provoked the jealousy of other Castilian knights who now conspired with Moorish enemies of Castile to lure El Cid to his death in a trap. However, the story goes that this plot failed, mainly because those Moorish kings whom El Cid had earlier spared and befriended warned Rodrigo of the danger and rallied to his aid in the nick of time. When King Ferdinand heard of this he also banished El Cid's enemies from the court of Castile.

At this point, unfortunately, King Ferdinand died leaving the kingdom of Castile to his eldest son Don Sancho, but charge of the provinces of Leon and Galicia to (respectively) Sancho's younger brothers Don Alfonso and Don Garcia, and of the wealthy cities of Zamora and Toro to his daughters, Doña Urrace and Doña Elvira. Given the contentious feudal temper of the times, here compounded by apparent hatred of Ferdinand's sons for one another, it was more or less inevitable that this divided inheritance would cause trouble—and no less certain that El Cid would be caught in the middle of it. It seems that Ferdinand's heirs were variously dissatisfied with their legacies—and Don Sancho himself seems to have had wider sovereign designs over the whole Spanish kingdom. Thus, suspecting attack sooner or later from various external and internal enemies, King Sancho was careful to keep El Cid on his side. The first threat came from the King of Navarre and Don Ramiro of Aragon whose invasion of Castile, soon after Sancho's accession, was easily repulsed by Rodrigo. But now, Don Garcia of Galicia, also anxious to increase his power and territory, took the city of Zamora from his sister Doña Urrac.

When Doña Urrace appealed to her brother Sancho for help, the king took his opportunity to wage war on Garcia and annex his kingdom. This turned into a larger family struggle when Don Alfonso joined Don Garcia in revolt against the king. While El Cid was unhappy about this family feud and opposed to civil war, he nevertheless supported Don Sancho and firmly crushed the rebels. Don Garcia died in prison while Don Alfonso escaped to join the Moors under their leader Alimaymon at Toledo.

All the same, inflated by his success and still greedy for more power and territory Don Sancho dispossessed Doña Elvira of Toro and laid siege to Doña Urrace's city of Zamora. While El Cid was unhappy with this situation, he agreed under protest to go to Doña Urrace to demand her surrender of Zamora. However, when Rodrigo returned with the message that Doña Urrace and the citizens of Zamora would die rather than surrender, Don Sancho angrily banished El Cid from his service. Still, realizing that El Cid's support was militarily indispensable to his ambitions, he recalled him to his service and Rodrigo renewed the siege of Zamora, now facing starvation. But events were soon to take a drastic turn when a citizen of Zamora came out of the town, and—under pretence of betraying the city into the king's hands—took the opportunity to assassinate King Sancho. Since Sancho had no offspring to succeed him, succession now fell to Don Alfonso who had taken refuge from Sancho with the Moors at Toledo—where he was now virtually a prisoner. Still, when Doña Urrace managed to get news of Don Sancho's death to Don Alfonso, he escaped from Toledo to return as the new king of Castile. Now, however, suspecting that Alfonso was instrumental in the murder of his brother, El Cid would not swear loyalty to the king unless Alfonso also swore that he had played no part in Sancho's death.

Smarting from what he took to be public humiliation of him, King Alfonso banished El Cid from the kingdom. While Rodrigo's exile was mourned by the Spanish people, to whom he was a popular hero, they were forbidden from aiding or sheltering him on pain of punishment by the king —though it was said that many persisted in doing so. However, leaving his beloved wife Ximena and two infant daughters in the care of others, El Cid was compelled to accept exile in the company of three hundred loyal followers. But again, in the wake of further expeditions and victories against the king's enemies, from which he sent spoils and presents back to Alfonso, Rodrigo was re-established in the favour of the king who sought his support in a long-time ambition to conquer the Moorish city of Toledo— which soon fell to El Cid's assault. Still, following a further quarrel between Alfonso and El Cid, which encouraged the Moors to take the coastal city of Valencia, Rodrigo returned to recapture this city and make it his own home and headquarters. Now master of Valencia, Rodrigo's daughters were given in marriage to King Alfonso's sons the Infantas (or royal princes) of Carrion. As chips off the old block, however, these princes seem to have proved generally disreputable and cowardly—especially in the face of a renewed Moorish attack on Valencia—and quickly became objects of derision and contempt to the people of the city.

So, following El Cid's heroic repulsion of the Moorish assault on Valencia, the despised princes of Carrion asked permission to return home with their brides with the many gifts received from El Cid. While anxious to see the back of his sons-in-law, El Cid was also reluctant to see his beloved daughters depart, but agreed to their going under the escort of one of his most loyal captains named Felez Muñoz. However, the princes, full of rancour and resentment for the contempt in which Rodrigo held them, resolved to take revenge. Their opportunity came, so the El Cid story goes, when they camped to break their journey to the court—and, early the next day, sent the rest of their retinue ahead promising to follow shortly with the two princesses. Instead, the princes severely beat Rodrigo's daughters leaving them for dead by the roadside, before riding off to re-join their escort. Fortunately, they were rescued by Felez Muñoz who hastened back to Valencia to inform El Cid of the violence — who, thirsting for revenge, rode straight to King Alfonso to demand justice. Apparently, even the gruesome Alfonso was appalled to hear how the princes had treated their wives, immediately summoning his sons to give account of themselves at the Spanish high court at Toledo. According to the story, the cowardly princes' efforts to justify their conduct on the ground that the daughters of El Cid were of too lowly birth to be fit wives for princes were rebutted when royal princes of Navarre — of allegedly far more noble blood — arrived at the court asking for the princesses' hands in marriage. But, in addition, El Cid also challenged the princes to meet him in armed combat, and — as we would only expect — gave them the thoroughly good thrashing they so richly deserved. The duly humiliated princes and their wicked uncle — since every good story needs a wicked uncle — were banished from the kingdom and El Cid returned in triumph to Valencia, where the second marriage of his daughters to the princes of Navarre also took place. Here El Cid was showered with honours from near and far — most notably from the Muslim Sultan of Persia who had also heard of his fame.

However, the most striking and colourful episode in the saga of El Cid is reserved for the conclusion of the story. Five years after the incident with the princes, the invading Moroccan King Bucar attempted to besiege Valencia. As was his wont, El Cid prepared to do battle with both Spanish and Moorish allies against an army of overwhelming odds — but was now visited by a vision of St Peter, telling him that he would die within thirty days. On the last of these — poisoned by an enemy arrow — Rodrigo was staring death in the face. Seeing that the words of this vision were about to be fulfilled, El Cid instructed that no one should proclaim his death lest the news should encourage the Moroccan invaders and discourage his followers. He directed that his embalmed body should be tied to the back of his famous steed Babieça, and that—with his equally renowned sword Tizona (the Excalibur of El Cid) fastened in his hand—he should ride against the enemy to certain victory. In accordance with his dying wishes, El Cid then rode posthumously into the fray at the head of his army, putting his Moorish enemies to fearful rout. At the order of King Alfonso, Rodrigo's body was placed in the church of San Pedro de Cardeña, where it remained for ten years seated in a chair of state as an object of respect and reverence. On this highly romantic note, so concludes the narrative of Rodrigo Diaz of Vivar, the legendary 'El Cid' of Vivar and Castile.

To be sure, while the El Cid narrative differs from that of Gareth in being apparently based on the life of an historical figure, it has also much of the mythological or archetypal character of Arthurian and other medieval epics and sagas. Whatever Rodrigo of Vivar may—as a matter of actual historical fact—have been like as a person, El Cid is of course the fantastically embroidered stuff of myth and legend. As such, so many elements of the story—the near magic swords and steeds, the mystical visions of saints, not to mention the moral perfection and virtual invincibility of the hero—cry out for less literal and more charitable moral and spiritual interpretation. In this regard, many of these elements (such as swords, steeds and visions)—also frequently encountered in Arthurian and other such narratives—are better interpreted as symbols of power, justice and sanctity. Clearly, however, one fairly distinctive emphasis of the El Cid story is that the moral virtues of honesty, courage, integrity, justice, compassion and piety—all of which El Cid is alleged to have possessed in abundance—are not necessarily if at all the product or inheritance of rank or privilege. Indeed, the narrative repeatedly emphasizes that, while Rodrigo is a knight, he is of relatively low birth or status and that all he achieves is accomplished through his own morally commendable character and effort. On the contrary, to be sure, the narrative bends over backwards to portray royalty and high status in the murkiest possible light. The ruling

Castilian dynasty is depicted as a viperous nest of vainglory, touchiness and treachery, and as clearly not to be trusted as far as anyone might throw them. While it is hard to believe that the story of the royal princes beating up the daughters of El Cid, to whom they are espoused, could be anything other than apocryphal—since the narrative is hardly credible given the wrath that any such action would have called down upon the perpetrators from our superhero—it nevertheless drives home the point that virtue and honour are not the stuff of easy inheritance and need to be earned. Just as clearly, it seems that this was a lesson that the powers and principalities of the day were most in need of learning. However, in relation to teaching about justice, particularly in contemporary contexts of cultural pluralism, the story of El Cid places remarkably early emphasis on the importance of respect and tolerance for people of other races and cultures —perhaps not least, in the contexts of many present day societies, for harmony and good relations between citizens of notably Christian and Muslim heritage.

Don Quixote (Miguel de Cervantes)

Like the El Cid narrative, the third of our knightly virtues stories takes us to Spain, though the leading actor in this drama is likely to be more widely familiar—or at least to have been heard of—than either Rodrigo Diaz or Gareth. To be sure, although a rather long and sprawling work (of over 400,000 words), it is likely that at least some episodes from Miguel de Cervantes' great comic masterpiece *Don Quixote* (Cervantes 1998) have featured in schoolroom collections of stories for children for some centuries. However, despite this fact—if not perhaps partly because of it—it may also be that it is now somewhat *passe* as a children's story and not much otherwise read (especially given its daunting length) by even educated adults. If so, such neglect is to be greatly lamented —since *Don Quixote* is not only one of the all-time greatest works of western European literature, and of early modern prose fiction in particular, but a work of profound moral and spiritual depth and significance for readers of all ages. However, the episodic structure of the narrative — which precisely lends itself to the easy isolation and extraction of such disconnected or self-standing comic episodes as Quixote's tilting at windmills or attacking herds of sheep — may also have served to obscure or belie the larger serious and/or tragic dimensions of the whole work as an extraordinarily profound reflection on the human search for value, meaning and purpose in a world in which such meaning and value is often hard to discern. Still, in *Don Quixote*, Cervantes addresses — with something more of the lighter comic touch of his great English contemporary William Shakespeare than the poker face of academic philosophy — profound questions that have exercised the very greatest thinkers at least since Plato.

On the face of it, *Don Quixote* is a comic tale of an ageing bachelor gentleman farmer named Alonso Quixada, whose imagination has been fired by the novels of knightly derring-do to which he has become addicted, and who sets out — in a rusting suit of armour, on a decrepit horse called Rocinante and accompanied by the portly peasant 'squire' Sancho Panza — to re-live or re-create the knightly quests of medieval chivalry. To his family and friends, it appears that Quixada has simply gone mad: as Don (Sir) Quixote, he takes inns and innkeepers for castles and kings, common peasant girls for noble ladies in distress, shaving bowls for magic helmets, windmills for giants, herds of sheep for armies of enemy knights and chained convicts as oppressed prisoners to be liberated. When the less romantic 'realities' behind Quixote's illusions (or delusions) are pointed out to him, he attributes the shifting appearance of things to the wiles of an evil 'enchanter' who engineers such changes of appearance and vision. On the face of it, it seems — and is often so characterizsed — that *Don Quixote* is a simple satire on or comic dismissal of the feudal ideals of medieval chivalry that were rapidly losing ground in Cervantes' time. But it is also fairly clear that Cervantes is also encouraging readers to view Quixote's 'madness' in a very much more sympathetic light than other characters in his story — inviting serious questions about the nature of madness and sanity, truth and illusion and virtue and vice. Still, we may postpone further general comment on this possibility until after we have given a brief overview of the tale.

At the beginning of the story, Alonso Quixada is an object of some concern to his family and friends who evidently think that the romances of knightly chivalry that he has lately been devouring have — in one fairly literal psychiatric sense — gone to his head. He is advised by all and sundry to submit to graceful retirement and to the tender care of his niece and housekeeper. No less strongly contemptuous of this advice, Alfonso determines to set out in pursuit of a knightly quest and plunders the house attic for equipment for this mission in the form of an ancient rusting suit of armour and an equally battered lance and shield. Assuming the title Don Quixote de la Mancha, he then mounts his no less ancient farm nag, renaming the horse Rocinante. Recalling that a true knight of chivalry should also dedicate himself to the service of a lady, he remembers a local village girl, honouring her with the imaginary title Dulcinea del Toboso. However, having already embarked upon his mission, he suddenly realizes that he has forgotten the most important item of all, the need to be knighted by a suitably appointed authority.

Reaching a miserable and neglected wayside inn, the self-styled Don Quixote apparently takes this to be a magnificent castle and accordingly addresses the innkeeper as the lord of the castle. Judging the old man to be not quite right in the head, the innkeeper decides to humour Don Quixote according to his fantasy. However, during supper at the inn, Quixote gets embroiled in a fight with other inn guests over a trivial difference with a muleteer, laying many of them out unconscious with his lance. Congratulating himself on this as the first of his heroic exploits, he then asks the innkeeper, as the imagined lord of the castle, to confer knighthood upon him. Fearful of further trouble if he refuses, the innkeeper falls in with this additional charade, dubbing Quixada the 'knight of the dolorous countenance' (or 'Sir long face)'. With this title, Don Quixote sallies forth to find a squire to assist his adventures. He soon happens upon the object of this new search in the portly shape of a peasant farmer, named Sancho Panza, who he persuades to accompany him by promises of adventure, spoils and booty.

The first adventure encountered by the famous literary comic double act of Don Quixote and Sancho Panza is probably one of the best known and loved episodes in literature. Whilst crossing a wide plain, Quixote indicates what he claims to be thirty terrifying giants with enormous arms, but which Sancho Panza recognizes as large windmills. Dismissing Sancho Panza's more mundane or prosaic interpretation of events, Quixote insists on engaging with the 'giants', charging at them with his lance. Caught in one of the windmill's sails, Quixote's lance is smashed to pieces and the knight errant is thrown from his horse onto the rough ground. When Sancho Panza again attempts to bring Quixote back to reality by pointing out that the so-called giants were actually windmills, the old man once more insists that it is Sancho who has got things wrong. According to Quixote, an evil enchanter has intervened to turn the giants into windmills in order to deprive him of the honour of a glorious victory. Proceeding their way on the following day, Don Quixote notices a huge cloud of dust on the road ahead and advises Sancho that this is a large army of enemy knights advancing on them. Once again, Sancho protests that this is only a herd of sheep, but Quixote ignores him and engages them in 'combat'. Protesting angrily at the scattered sheep, the shepherds pelt Quixote with stones, and the would-be knight again bites the dust with loss of some dental repair. Again, Quixote refuses to be persuaded by Sancho's insistence that the alleged knights were only sheep and continues to claim that they had been transformed into sheep by his arch-enemy the evil enchanter.

Don Quixote and Sancho Panza next encounter twelve men walking in a line, shackled together on a great iron chain — obviously convicts — in the charge of four guards, two on horseback and two on foot. Again, while Sancho advises Quixote that these are criminal elements being led to penal service in the galleys, the old man insists that they are innocents enslaved against their own will by the forces of tyranny. Despite the fact that, when questioned by him, the convicts freely admit to having broken the law, Quixote, provoked by the taunts of the guards, sets about them, and — with the reluctant help of a terrified Sancho — puts them to flight. Quixote then announces to the prisoners that he is giving them their liberty and asks them in return to report his gallantry to his beloved Dulcinea de Toboso. Unsurprisingly, the convicts take their 'liberator' to be an imbecile, beat a hasty retreat before the police can arrive to re-arrest them and — to Quixote's evident surprise and dismay — show their gratitude by stealing his coat and Sancho's hat.

On the next stage of their adventure, also hoping to evade possible pursuit by the police, Don Quixote and Sancho leave the beaten track to follow a mountain forest trail and stumble across a bag hidden in a pile of leaves. Sancho opens this to find four shirts, gold coins and an old notebook containing a poem that runs: 'Where gods are cruel and love is blind / Misery has pierced my mind / Let me die, for I am sure / Without Lucinda, there's no cure.' Donating the gold coins to a grateful Sancho, Quixote surmises that the poem has been written by a lovelorn knight retiring to the forest to die of unrequited passion. At this point, a wild man with long hair and bushy beard appears, begging for food. Welcoming him, Quixote invites him to eat and tell his story. The man introduces himself as Cardenio, a nobleman from Andalusia, who is in love with a young woman named Lucinda — whose father granted them permission to marry. However, a powerful Spanish noble named Duke Ricardo demanded Cardenio's services as a companion to his son, Fernando, who was also attracted to

Lucinda. As Ferdinand's family was richer than Cardenio's, her father was persuaded that Ferdinand should be Lucinda's husband. This is why Cardenio ran off into the mountain wilderness.

Quixote is shocked by this story and worried that he may be in for some such disappointment from his favoured lady Dulcinea del Toboso. In this spirit, he pens the following lines to her: 'Noble Lady, Sweetest Dulcinea del Toboso, If your beautiful self scorns me, my life is not worth living / Say you will be mine, or I will end it — to satisfy your cruelty and my desire / Your own, Knight of the Long Face' — and instructs Sancho to deliver these to the wench so titled. Having no intention of delivering the letter, but glad to escape for a hot dinner, Sancho makes for an inn where he is surprised to bump into Quixote's friends the priest and the barber from La Mancha — who, naturally, interrogate him concerning the old man's whereabouts. Sancho explains the turn of events so far and shows them Quixada's letter to Dulcinea. While they have little interest in the letter, the priest and barber are very concerned to find Quixote and return him to the safety of his own home. Sancho therefore leads them to where he last left Quixote, re-encountering Cardenio along the way and then running across what seems to be a young farmer's lad paddling in a river and singing a sad song. This turns out to be a maiden in disguise named Dorotea, who seems to have been jilted by Ferdinand for Lucinda. Dorotea reports Lucinda as having said that she only agreed to marry Ferdinand under pressure from her parents and that she really only loved Cardenio. Cardenio now declares that his madness is cured and that he will not rest until he is reunited with Lucinda and Dorotea is married to Ferdinand. However, hearing from the priest that his first concern is to take care of Don Quixote, Dorotea comes up with an ingenious plan.

Asking the barber to find her a pretty dress, the party discovers Don Quixote sitting under a tree and Dorotea throws herself at his feet. She then declares that she is the

Princess Micomicona, whose land has been stolen by an ogre who has also threatened to eat her father, and she implores the old man's knightly aid. Drawn by the prospect of rescuing 'a beautiful damsel in distress', Quixote rises to the bait and allows himself to be led by Dorotea to a nearby inn. Closely following them, the barber and the priest advise the innkeeper not to be alarmed by the deluded Quixote who is then offered a place to sleep in the loft of the inn. In the middle of the night there is a tremendous commotion and Quixote is discovered laying about him with his sword — much to the chagrin of the innkeeper — at the stored inn wine sacks which he has taken to be Princess Micomicona's 'giant'. Declaring that the room is too sodden with blood — in reality the spilled wine — to sleep in, Quixote goes downstairs where he is seized by two ghostly figures with white faces and dark cloaks and thrown, with Sancho, into a wooden cage mounted on an ox cart. In scary voices, the figures extract a promise from Quixote not to embark on any more adventures for a year. Taking off their disguises, the priest and the barber then proceed to take Don Quixote back home to La Mancha.

Shortly afterwards, Don Quixote wakes up to find himself back at home in his own bed, in the care of his niece and housekeeper who are relieved to have him returned safely. Feeling weak, the old man dimly recalls his knightly adventures with Sancho and Rocinante. When Sancho comes to visit him, he declares that he is now famous and shows him a large book illustrated with pictures of Quixote on Rocinante, tilting at windmills and charging at sheep. However, the squire is also unhappy with the publication, since it seems to make Don Quixote into a figure of fun. He insists that this does not tell the truth about Don Quixote the noble, heroic and courageous champion of truth, justice and honour. Quixote complains that he does not feel well and asks for a priest and doctor — and, when the doctor arrives, his verdict is that Quixote is stricken with acute melancholia. The old man now insists that he is no longer Don Quixote de la Mancha, but rather Alonso Quixada, avowing that, though previously mad, he has now recovered his sanity. Ignoring Sancho's distraught attempts to rally his spirits by proposing new adventures, the old man now makes his will, leaving his wealth and possessions to his niece, housekeeper and Sancho, and gives up the ghost. His friends have the following obituary written on his gravestone: 'Don Quixote: He never cared what people thought / A clown to pompous eyes / He lived his life a gallant fool / And finally died wise.

The last touching moments of the narrative—not least Sancho's tearful defence of the 'true' Don Quixote—are evidently to the real point of the story. It seems that the key question that the story raises is that of whether Quixote—taken by the world to be mad—has not attained a kind of sanity or wisdom that the world in its own madness and delusion has failed to grasp. From this viewpoint, it is Quixote who is really the 'enchanter', who constantly aspires to transform everything ordinary and/or tawdry into something magical, dignified and noble. Indeed, Don Quixote possesses all the knightly virtues of his enchanted vision: he is truly courageous in his assault on the windmill 'giants'; he is genuinely courteous in his treatment of all 'ladies' regardless of their actual social station; he shows true justice in attempting to liberate others from what he takes to be their oppression; he is (by contrast with Sancho Panza) really temperate in taking no more food or drink than his basic needs; and he is unfailingly generous in giving to others any material gains that fortune sends his way. Indeed, the deathbed scenes of the book, in which Sancho Panza—who at the outset seems to have regarded the Quixotic quest as no more than a crazy joke—tries to persuade Quixada to return to the life of knightly adventure that has given real meaning to his own life, are amongst the most moving in literature. It seems that while Quixote's life is a comedy, his death is a great tragedy—since, with his passing, so passes enchantment, idealism and true nobility of spirit from the world. In this connection, a good question to pursue with young readers or audiences of this work might be: *Most of the other characters in the story seem to regard Quixote as a fool or a madman: is this what the author thinks or wants us to believe?* As a further aid to imaginative reflection on this question, there are some reasonable movie versions of Quixote (including one with Peter O'Toole and Sophia Loren) from which useful illustrative clips might be taken.

The Merchant of Venice (William Shakespeare)

To be sure, it is probably invidious and unhelpful to try to rank authors in terms of stature. Still, if the author of *Don Quixote* is one of the giants of western literature, it is hardly an exaggeration to say that the reputation as such of his English contemporary William Shakespeare is just as if not more widespread on the global literary stage. As earlier indicated, it has often been held that the two main sources of western literature — certainly in English — are the Bible and Shakespeare. Again, as already noticed, Shakespeare's plays are also full of memorable explorations of good and bad character, and — insofar as the Jubilee Knightly Virtues project was inspired by the idea that knights of old might be considered paragons of virtue and chivalry — one might expect to find plenty of such examples in the works of the Bard of Avon. Curiously, however, many of the knightly characters in Shakespeare are flawed or tragic figures who do not readily fit the required bill: the lives and exploits of Macbeth, Othello and Coriolanus (for example) are marred by various character shortcomings or vices and one of the most memorable of actual Shakespearean knights — Sir John Falstaff — is (as seen in the plays of *Henry IV* and *V* and in *The Merry Wives of Windsor*) the epitome of dissolution and debauchery. However, in light of one aforementioned serious deficit of the Jubilee project — the obvious gender bias of any focus on knights — Shakespeare comes to the rescue with an impressive array of highly virtuous heroines. And while there were so many here to choose from, it was decided for the purposes of the project to focus on Portia in *The Merchant of Venice* (Shakespeare 2005).

This play opens with a conversation between Antonio, a successful merchant, and his friend Bassanio: the latter seems distracted and Antonio presses him to explain the reason for his melancholy mood. Bassanio relates that he recently met a beautiful young woman named Portia in the town of Belmont and has fallen in love with her. He had also recently heard that Portia's father had died, leaving her an enormous fortune. When Antonio urges Bassanio to lose no time in seeking Portia's hand in marriage, Bassanio laments that he is too poor to compete with other suitors and would need at least three thousand ducats to do so. Antonio says that he would be happy to give the money to his friend for this purpose, but regrets that his capital is currently all tied up in various seaborne enterprises. However, Antonio assures Bassanio that he is still creditworthy and willing to take a loan on interest to fund him in his romantic quest, and the latter happily accepts this offer. Shortly afterwards, Bassanio approaches a Jewish moneylender named Shylock for the loan of three thousand ducats on Antonio's pledge, promising him that the money will be paid back with interest within three months.

Antonio now joins them and endorses the deal that Bassanio has proposed to Shylock. It is immediately clear that Antonio and Shylock have no love for one another. When Antonio repeats Bassanio's request for the loan, Shylock expresses or feigns some surprise, since the merchant has often declared his contempt for money lending and usurers. However, Antonio points out that he is making an exception in this case only to help his friend. With barely concealed ire, Shylock reminds Antonio of the times when Antonio has assaulted him, spat upon him and expressed contempt for both his (Jewish) race and money lending profession. At a later point in the play, indeed, Shylock makes a very memorable speech—appealing for justice and retribution in the teeth of racial discrimination and hatred — which is here worth quoting at length:

> He [Antonio] hath disgraced me and hindered me half a million; laughed at my losses, mocked at my gains, scorned my nation, thwarted my bargains, cooled my friends, heated mine enemies! And what's his reason? I am a Jew! Hath not a Jew eyes? Hath not a Jew hands, organs, dimensions, senses, affections, passions? Fed with the same food, hurt with the same weapons, subject to the same diseases, healed by the same means, warmed and cooled by the same winter and summer as a Christian is? If you prick us, do we not bleed? If you tickle us, do we not laugh? If you poison us, do we not die? And if you wrong us, shall we not revenge? (*The Merchant of Venice*, Act 1, scene 3, lines 49–61)

Antonio admits that there is no love lost between them and comments that it should therefore please Shylock to be in a position to charge him for the loan. This appears to amuse the moneylender who then states that the only penalty he will impose on the loan is that — in the event of default by Antonio at the end of the three month period — the merchant will agree to Shylock's cutting a pound of flesh from a place on his body nearest his heart. While Bassanio is horrified at this and pleads with Antonio not to agree, the merchant takes it as a dare — since he may be accused of cowardice if he refuses — and promises to abide by Shylock's terms. Ignoring Shylock's obvious satisfaction at this, he assures Bassanio that his ships will return to Venice within a month and that all will be well.

Meanwhile, in Belmont, the lady Portia is exercised by an unwelcome imposition. Her father has stated, as a condition of his will, that any suitors for Portia's hand in marriage should be made to choose between three caskets — one made of gold, another of silver and the third made of lead: the will states that Portia will have to be wife to whichever suitor picks the right casket. While reminding Portia that this was a condition of inheritance of her father's wealth, her maid Nerissa teases her with the memory of Bassanio, who she knows would be the suitor of Portia's choice. Although Portia offers some embarrassed protest to this suggestion, it is clear that she is no less drawn to Bassanio than he to her. However, Portia is nevertheless obliged to welcome her first suitor, the Prince of Morocco, to the room where the caskets are kept. The handsome prince examines the caskets, picks up the one made of lead, and reads the inscription: 'If you choose me, you must risk all that you have.' The prince then puts down the casket, saying dismissively that he will not risk all for lead. The silver casket has the inscription: 'If you choose me, you will get as much as you deserve.' While quipping that this could be the casket—since, after all, Portia is the best and he deserves the best—he turns to the inscription on the gold casket, which says: 'If you choose me you will get what many men desire.' He decides that this must be the one—since Portia is the most desirable of women, but is horrified on opening it to find that the casket contains a human skull with a parchment that reads: 'All that glisters is not gold / As you often have been told / You have chosen outward show / So now say farewell, and go.' To Portia's relief, the prince exits without a further word.

The next afternoon, the Prince of Aragon arrives to try his luck with Portia's three caskets. Rejecting the lead casket as too base and unworthy and the golden one as a bit too obvious, he chooses the silver one. However, when he opens it, he finds a miniature painting of a man dressed as a jester. The accompanying parchment scroll reads: 'This picture makes it plain to see / That you have chosen foolishly / Though you are strong, your mind is weak / And you are not the one I seek.' Like his Moroccan colleague, the prince pays his respects to Portia and leaves. At this point, however, Nerissa bursts into the room to announce excitedly that the next awaiting suitor is none other than Bassanio. While Portia is no less excited as Nerissa, she declares that he will have to take the casket test like the others. Still, Bassanio enters to Portia's delight and she explains the conditions of her father's will. In turn, Bassanio admits that he is poor and relates how and why Antonio had borrowed money from Shylock. Despite a nervous request from Portia to delay taking the test — since she is afraid that if he chooses wrongly she will never see him again — Bassanio insists on being led to the caskets. Examining them in turn, he declares that the lead casket appears to hide nothing through show, and he opens it. Inside is a portrait of Portia and a scroll that reads: 'You have not chosen with your eyes / But with your heart, and you are wise / Turn now to where the lady is / And claim her with a loving kiss.'

Overjoyed that he has passed the test, Portia takes a ring from her finger and asks Bassanio never to part with it as long as he loves her and he swears never to take it off as long as he might live. So Bassanio and Portia are happily married and Portia's maidservant Nerissa is also married to Bassanio's manservant Gratiano. However, as blissful married weeks turn into months, Bassanio forgets about Antonio's loan until at breakfast one morning, he receives a letter from Venice. He there reads with horror that Antonio's ships have been lost at sea, that Shylock has had him thrown into prison and — worse yet — that the moneylender is demanding his debt of the pound of flesh. When Portia suggests buying Shylock off with twice the debt if he wishes, Bassanio informs her that Shylock's daughter Jessica has run off and married a Christian, taking money from her father's cash boxes — all of which has hardened the Jew's heart against Antonio. However, Portia insists that since they owe all their happiness to Antonio's help, Bassanio should hasten to see and support his friend at the earliest opportunity.

While Bassanio prepares to do this, Portia calls Nerissa and tells her the story of Antonio, saying that she is going to help him. She relates that her cousin, Dr Bellario, had taught her something of law when she had tried to understand her father's will and that she will call him for a letter of introduction to the Duke of Venice to discuss Antonio's case. She proposes that she and Nerissa should then go to the court disguised as lawyers. On the day of Antonio's trial, the Duke of Venice sits in the judge's chair with Shylock to his left, and Antonio and Bassanio to his right. After demanding silence, the Duke asks for the lawyer Balthazar, sent by Dr Bellario to defend Antonio, and – disguised in lawyers' robes – Portia and Nerissa stand up and bow. When the Duke asks Portia to start the proceedings, she begins by asking Shylock if he would release Antonio from his bond if the latter returned the three thousand ducats he had borrowed. Shylock replies that he would not do this for sixty thousand ducats. Having ascertained from Antonio that he had not been tricked into signing the bond, she then declares it legal, but nevertheless asks for mercy from Shylock. When Shylock asks why he should be merciful, Portia explains that mercy brings blessings, both to those who receive it and those who give it. Again, Portia's mercy speech at this point is one of the most famous in Shakespeare.

> The quality of mercy is not strain'd; it droppeth as the gentle rain from heaven upon the place beneath; it is twice bless'd; it blesseth him that gives and him that takes; 'tis mightiest in the mightiest; it becomes the thron'd monarch better than his crown; his sceptre shows the force of temporal power, the attribute to awe and majesty, wherein doth sit the dread and fear of kings; but mercy is above this sceptred sway. – it is an attribute to God himself; and earthly power doth then show likest God's when mercy seasons justice. (*The Merchant of Venice*, Act 4, scene 1, lines 182–194)

When Shylock insists that he desires justice not blessing, Portia asks to examine the bond between him and Antonio. When the clerk of the court hands her the bond, she declares that the bond is legal, that Shylock is within his rights and Antonio should bare his breast and prepare to die. Shylock produces a dagger that he then proceeds to sharpen on a small stone. But now Portia advises that he should be careful where to cut, since the bond specifies only that a pound of Antonio's *flesh* might be cut from the place closest to his heart, but does not mention blood. She insists that should Shylock shed a drop of Antonio's blood, the state of Venice will prosecute him and confiscate all his possessions. Realizing that he has been tricked, Shylock now tries to demand repayment of his three thousand ducats, but Portia points out that he has already refused the money in open court. The Duke now steps in and advises Shylock that, according to the laws of Venice, his effective attempt on Antonio's life warrants confiscation of half his property to the state, the other half to be given to the intended victim. Realizing he is ruined, Shylock says that the court might as well have sentenced him to death. Portia now asks if Antonio is inclined to show Shylock any mercy and the merchant pronounces that the moneylender may keep his half of his property, so long as he agrees to become a Christian. On this note, the Duke closes the proceedings.

A relieved Bassanio hastens to Portia, still disguised as the lawyer Balthazar, and promises anything she or 'he' might ask for saving his friend Antonio's life. At this Portia asks him for the gold ring she had given him at the time of their wedding. Although the distraught Bassanio pleads that this is his wedding ring, Portia insists on holding him to his promise to give her anything she wants. Antonio adds his voice to this for the services that Portia, alias 'Balthazar', has rendered him and, reluctantly, Bassanio gives up the ring to Portia. In addition, the 'clerk' Nerissa who had also given her husband a wedding ring, begs it from Gratian and he duly surrenders it to her. After the men have departed, Portia and Nerissa laugh together, reflecting on how, when they get home, they will taunt their husbands about giving away their rings. Hence, when Bassanio arrives home to tell Portia the good news about Antonio's escape from the Shylock threat, they both perceive Nerissa and Gratiano quarrelling in a corner of the room. When Portia asks Gratiano the reason for the quarrel, he confesses it is about the missing ring that Nerissa is accusing him of having given to another woman.

Gratiano insists that he gave it to the clerk of the young counsellor who saved Antonio's life. Portia now chides

Gratiano for parting with the ring and insists that her husband Bassanio would never have done such a thing. Anxious to get out of the hot seat, however, Gratiano blabs that his master Bassanio has also given away his ring to the counsellor. Feigning anger, Portia now turns on Bassanio for giving away her ring, also accusing him of giving it to some other woman. Much upset, Bassanio protests that he gave the ring to the lawyer who saved Antonio. Antonio now turns up to confirm his story, insisting to Portia that Bassanio surely did well to give the lawyer what he asked for by way of repayment for saving his friend's life. Portia now feigns forgiveness of Bassanio offering another ring to look after more carefully than the last. When Bassanio looks at this ring, he recognizes it as the one he had given away, and realizes that his wife was the wise young 'counsellor' who had saved Antonio's life. Portia again welcomes Antonio, also giving him further good news that his ships had not been lost at sea but safely reached Venice's harbour. The play thus concludes on a light note with much comic banter over the husbands who could not even recognize their own wives. In the bard's own words, spoken by Portia to the general company and Antonio:

> Here is a letter, read it at your leisure; it comes from Padua, from Bellario: there you shall find that Portia was the doctor; Nerissa there, her clerk; Lorenzo here shall witness I set forth as soon as you, and but even now return'd; I have not yet enter'd my house—Antonio. You are welcome; and I have better news in store for you than you expect; unseal this letter soon; there you shall find three of your argosies are richly come to harbour suddenly; you shall not know by what strange accident I chanced on this letter. (*The Merchant of Venice*, Act 5, scene 1, lines 67–77)

As stated in the introduction to this section, Shakespeare's *The Merchant of Venice* was selected as a key work for the Knightly Virtues project because it does something to redress the gender imbalance of exclusive focus on heroic males, and also perhaps provides an opportunity for attention to gentler or more feminine virtues — although we do not take the view in this project that virtues are generally divisible along gender lines. But what is certainly conspicuous in this play — as in quite a number of Shakespeare's dramas — is the much more favourable light in which female characters often appear by contrast with their male counterparts. Indeed, if ever anyone was inclined to doubt Shakespeare's feminist sympathies (leaving aside perhaps *The Taming of the Shrew* and *Macbeth*) then *King Lear, Othello, A Winter's Tale, Measure for Measure, The Merry Wives of Windsor, The Merchant of Venice* and many other plays — all of which depict women as caring, steadfast and wise and men as for the most part foolish, gullible and prey to their own lower appetites and instincts — should do much to set them straight. In this light, *The Merchant of Venice* seems a fairly clear study of the calm decency and common sense of the heroines Portia, Jessica, but also to some extent Nerissa, with whom the likes of Antonio, Bassanio and Shylock compare very unfavourably.

The first of these — Antonio the merchant — is clearly depicted from the outset as impetuous, arrogant, racist and reckless. Bassanio is no less prone to act without thinking and also appears — like Romeo in another much loved Shakespearean drama — to have his head in some cloud of romantic folly. Thus, apart from his flash of inspiration in choosing the right casket, one might wonder quite what Portia sees in him. Finally, on the male side, Shylock — with whom one may have some sympathy for the way he seems to have been victimized (albeit evidently smarter and more down to earth than his Christian tormentors) — has nevertheless evidently abandoned any better self to which he might have aspired in pursuit of twisted, spiteful and sadistic revenge. It is above all Portia who keeps a clear head in a crisis, shows herself capable of wise and compassionate judgement and who is also the main spokesperson in the play for the higher human virtues of truth, justice and mercy. At all events, irrespective of any and all alignment of virtue or vice with particular genders, the play clearly presents an excellent opportunity to study the nature and operations of what Aristotle regarded as the master virtue of moral character—namely *phronesis* or practical wisdom—as a moral panacea for some of the worst vices of *hubris*, vanity, resentment, folly and delusion to which human flesh is heir.

Implementation of the Knightly Virtues Programme

Background to the Programme

As lately seen, the aim of the Knightly Virtues programme was to try to promote deeper understanding of notions of moral virtue and good character on the part of upper primary pupils (stages 5 and 6) in a variety of British schools via exploration of the classic stories described and discussed in the last chapter. The programme and supporting teaching materials were developed over the course of a year by a mixed group of theorists and practitioners, including various academics from the University of Birmingham, head-teachers, teachers and young people themselves. The four key stories of *Gareth and Lynette*, *El Cid*, *Don Quixote* and *The Merchant of Venice* were selected—following protracted discussion and deliberation—from a much longer list of thirty or so initially proposed possibilities. As already indicated, it was hoped—given the time-honoured appeal of all these stories—that there would be something in all of them to attract the interest of today's young people irrespective of gender. While all four stories were adapted or rewritten with a view to rendering them accessible to an 9–11 year-old readership or audience—a process that involved some consultation with head-teachers, classroom teachers and pupils themselves—care was also taken to ensure that there was no undue 'dumbing-down' of either content or presentation and that, in particular, some flavour of the original language in which the stories had been written was preserved in the rewriting. Indeed, irrespective of other significant moral educational objectives of the Knightly Virtues project, the architects of this project recognized the inherent educational merit of exposure of young people to culturally significant literature of the kind represented by all these classic stories.

That said, given the main aim of the Knightly Virtues project to promote deeper understanding of virtues and qualities of moral character, the four stories were re-written with a view to foregrounding the moral virtues—and vices—exhibited by the main characters of the narratives. Moreover, while all four of these stories clearly offer rich opportunities for exploration of a range of virtues (and/or vices), it was decided for strategic reasons to concentrate on one or two of the more conspicuous moral character traits shown in each of the stories. For reasons that may now be apparent from the discussions of the previous chapter, the moral virtues or character traits chosen for special attention in each of the four narratives were those shown in the table below.

Story	Featured Virtues
Gareth and Lynette	Courage, Humility
El Cid	Humility, Honesty
Don Quixote	Love, Service
Merchant of Venice	Self-discipline, Justice, Gratitude

Still, from a more logistical perspective, the Knightly Virtues project presented a number of challenges, to which the present chapter will give more particular attention under two main headings. The first of these—which we may here call the *pedagogical* problem—was precisely that of how to present or teach the four key narratives on the rough ground of actual classroom practice. More precisely, this was the problem of what methods of instruction might be adopted, or teaching resources developed, for the most effective communication of the moral significance of such stories to pupils in contemporary schools. However, the second challenge—which we may here call the *curriculum* problem —was that of how to fit the Knightly Virtues programme into the existing structures and patterns of formal curricular provision of contemporary British state or other primary schooling. For here, while it cannot be denied that primary schools have often formerly employed stories for a variety of educational or other purposes—or that moral education in some form or other has always featured in the school curricula of early and primary years—the explicit use of classic stories for purposes of learning about moral character breaks new ground at least to the extent of not fitting readily or neatly into the boxes of existing British primary curricular provision. From this viewpoint, as we shall see, it was not always clear to the teachers in schools where they might or could accommodate the Knightly Virtues programme in their (officially) prescribed daily educational agendas, practices and routines. However, we may return to this issue after we have first given some account of the pedagogical approach or approaches of the programme and of the development of supporting materials and resources.

The Teaching Materials

In general, a teaching pack—including notes for teachers, student journals and other accompanying resources—was assembled for all participants in the Knightly Virtues project. The pack sought to provide fairly detailed advice for teachers about how to deliver the five lessons outlined in the programme with particular regard to the sort of issues and problems that one might expect to be raised and/or addressed in professional teaching plans. Thus, the pack attempts to identify the most effective learning and teaching strategies for clear comprehension of the historical context and narrative structure of each of the stories as well as activities conducive to pupil recognition and grasp of the key virtues (and/or vices) exhibited by the main protagonists of the narratives. In the now professionally approved and prescribed — if controversial — language of teacher professionalism, the teachers' pack also indicates or suggests possible educational objectives or learning outcomes of the programme (with some reference to National Curriculum guidelines), and contains advice for possible assessment of the programme.

The Journal

Apart from the teachers themselves, however, by far the most important teaching and learning resource of the Knightly Virtues project is the *journal*, which each and every pupil is given on entry to the programme. In the first place, the Knightly Virtues journal includes the basic texts of all four key narratives so that these may be read or re-read by pupils at any time they wish, as an aid to completion of the various set learning tasks, or just simply for enjoyment. Moreover, since the literary abilities of the participating 9–11 pupils in the various schools employing the programme ranged quite widely, having their own copy of the story allowed them to follow the stories when these were read to them, and/or to add their own notes on meaning and interpretation as and when required. Each story was also provided with a glossary of key virtue and other terms to help pupils less familiar with such language to follow or grasp the overall drift of the narratives.

In addition to initial or provisional definitions or glosses of key virtue (and other) terms, however, the journal includes activities designed to encourage young people to engage in deeper reflection on the key character traits, their personal and social significance and their relevance to or implications for their own lives and conduct. In this regard, the journal invites pupils to create story boards, cartoons and pictures related to the main characters of the narratives and provides opportunities for self-evaluation or Assessment for Learning (AfL) following specific lessons. To be sure, insofar

as the key learning activities of the Knightly Virtues programme are actually contained in the journal and completed
by pupils in their own personal copies, they also give a very
accurate record of individual pupil learning. As already indicated, the journals were originally designed and developed
in consultation with pupils to try to ensure their appeal for
young people of the target age groups. Further to this, in
addition to employing a variety of illustrations for attractive
visual effect, parchment-textured paper was used for the
front cover to give a distinctive 'antiquated' or old-fashioned
feel to the journals.

Including the main programme activities in the journals
is also conducive to individualized learning insofar as it
allows pupils to work through activities at their own pace. In
this connection, pupils are from the outset encouraged to
individualize journals with their own personal details, notes
and pictures. To be sure, this personalized approach is also
meant to reinforce a key lesson of the project that the aim of
the programme is not to *tell* pupils what is morally right or
wrong, but to encourage authentic or autonomous exploration of the deep moral complexities of virtue and virtue discourse precisely through their own personal engagement
with the stories. Precisely, the aim of the Knightly Virtues
programme is to foster pupils' powers of moral reason and
deliberation as potential authors of their own characters, and
so to appreciate that the growth of virtue is not simply a
matter of social conformity or doing what others tell one to
do, but of serious and responsible reflection on what is
morally right or wrong—not least in morally conflicted
circumstances. To this end, the four basic narratives of the
Knightly Virtues programme were chosen precisely because
of their evident potential for profound reflection upon the
respects in which genuine virtue or moral character is frequently at odds with customary, conventional or received
ways of thinking about moral life and association.

In this regard, the warning of Lockwood (2009)—that
some latter day programmes of character education have

over-emphasized role modelling, habituation and/or obedience to authority at the expense of understanding *why* this prescribed conduct is to be regarded as 'better' than that—is mostly timely. From this viewpoint, one large problem of moral educational theorizing is that of developing opportunities or strategies for the development of moral dispositions that are both reflective and authentic—in the sense of appropriately internalized or 'taken to heart'. In this regard, the key question is that of precisely how one might aid the growth of those capacities for experientially engaged moral reason—in the absence of immediate personal involvement in a given moral predicament—of the sort that Aristotle identified with the experiential wisdom of *phronesis*. To be sure, past and present-day schools have often employed a wide range of educational strategies and techniques that might well assist such personal self-reflection: such strategies have included debates, discussions, philosophical enquiry sessions and so on. Still, while the value of such activities for more engaged moral self-reflection should not be underestimated, it may be that journals provide a more personal and private space for such reflection that is not so readily available in the contexts of such more public activities. In this regard, Hallberg and others claim that reflective writing in the form of a personal journal is 'person making': that 'journals are far more powerful and far-reaching in their effects than is generally recognised'; and that they 'change student's enduring attitudes, values and sense of personal identity' (Hallberg 1987, p. 289). If this is so, the Knightly Virtues journals may be regarded as a pedagogically effective vehicle of such deep personal exploration of the relevance of the project stories to pupils' own lives and for the exercise of some moral reflection and deliberation with regard to these. Insofar, the Knightly Virtues journal—explicitly focused as it is on moral themes and issues—might be considered a step further on the path to development of the all-important capacity, character trait or virtue of *phronesis* or practical wisdom.

At all events, there can be no doubt that the personal journals have been exceptionally well received in schools and regarded by both teachers and pupils as the most successful and enjoyable features of the Knightly Virtues programme. Thus, contrasting the use of journals with what happens in 'normal' literacy lessons, one primary 5 boy remarked: 'I like having my own journal because in literacy you just do it with a piece of paper… but this is like a diary, a journal you can keep; you can put what you want and you can do it on your own.' Similarly, a primary 6 girl observed that it seemed possible to learn more through the journals, and commented: 'I would rather read the stories in the journal than like the ones that we have in school, because like they have morals and it's just more nicer to read.' Appreciation of the many positive educational aspects of the journals has also been forthcoming from teachers. Thus, commenting on how much the pupils valued the personal character of their journals, one teacher remarked:

> I love the little journals and the kids themselves like them; I know if I was at school, I'd have loved to have had one of those. Yes, they really, they really liked them and they think it was nice having that book; and it was theirs, and they were a really nice aspect of the programme.

Another teacher observed:

> The children love the journals because it's personalized. It's their own one, they put their name in it, they draw a picture of themselves and then they feel that they own it. So that's a great start to the programme.

Other Teaching Materials

In addition to the journal, however, a variety of other aids and resources are included in the teaching pack to support delivery of the Knightly Virtues programme — including, notably, a PowerPoint slideshow for each of the five lessons of the programme. The slideshow features film clips, crucial historical background to the four key narratives as well as other (visual and other) aids to stimulate pupil interest in the programme. Other additional resources for teaching the programme — such as games cards, story cards, pictures and posters — are also contained in the pack. Such resources also contain advice or recommendations for further activities that might generally extend pupil learning, suggestions for differentiated learning in the light of individual differences and useful links to other resources or activities that might support teaching and learning.

The Curriculum

Still, the other large problem facing actual practical implementation of the Knightly Virtues programme — especially for teachers — was that of finding an appropriate place or places to fit this within official UK primary curriculum provision. Such provision is remarkably complex and subject to bewildering historically conditioned national, regional and local variations to which we cannot here do full justice. For now, it must suffice to say something about the general outlines of — and differences between — the two most presently relevant nationally/regionally dominant UK requirements or guidelines for primary educational provision of England and Scotland. Briefly, while still requiring the daily act of (albeit nowadays largely non-confessional) worship of early post-WWII heritage, the English (Welsh and Northern Irish) national curriculum for primary schools specifies twelve 'subjects' of study: three of these — namely English, Mathematics and Science — are labelled 'core'; and the remaining nine — namely Art and Design, Citizenship, Computing, Design and Technology, Languages, History, Music, Physical Education — are designated 'foundational'. In addition, the curriculum prescribes teaching of Religious Education (in some broad culturally inclusive form) for all key stages. On the other hand, the present day Scottish school curriculum (*Curriculum for Excellence*) has inherited — from the Scottish *Primary Memorandum* of the nineteen sixties — a much less subject-centred and more 'progressive' or integrated curricular approach that currently includes Expressive Arts, Health and Well-being, Languages, Mathematics, Religious and Moral Education, Sciences, Social Studies and Technologies, as somewhat less discrete or 'pigeon-holed' areas or domains of educational experience. There are therefore some fairly conspicuous differences between the two curricular models: thus, citizenship education in Scotland is treated as a cross-curricular rather than as an additional 'bolt-on' subject as in England; Scottish physical education is included in 'Health and Well-being' rather than treated as a separate 'subject' as in England; religious education in Scotland is included under the broader heading of 'Religious and Moral Education' rather than as a separate subject as in England; and (presumably) historical learning in Scotland is distributed across other areas of educational concern rather than occurring as a separate subject as in England. Still, it seems generally safe to say that the promotion of basic skills of literacy and numeracy, through the subjects or 'experiences' of English or 'Language' and Mathematics, are high official educational priorities in both Scotland and England.

As already seen, the Knightly Virtues is a programme that has (to date) aimed to provide school pupils of 9 to 11 years with the opportunity for imaginative or creative exploration of time-honoured (at least in western culture) stories of knights and heroes, for the purpose of personally formative learning about the moral significance and implications of virtue as character. To this end, the programme follows a series of five lessons. In each of the first four of these, the pupils read — or have read to them — one of the stories and are then given some space to reflect upon and/or discuss the virtues (or vices) of the key characters of the story. In the fifth and final lesson, pupils are invited to reflect on all four stories with regard to their possible relevance to or implications for their own personal character development. However, while the Knightly Virtues programme was designed to be as adaptable as possible to the national, regional and local curriculum priorities and requirements of British schools, the difficulties of accommodating non-standard educational programmes such as the Knightly Virtues character education project within the received curricular fare and time constraints of primary schooling should not be underestimated. More precisely, while character education of the kind advocated by the Knightly Virtues project is widely regarded as beneficial by many educational theorists, schools and teachers, the problem persists of where such 'extra' educational frills or 'luxuries' might go without serious disruption of official requirements and constraints often informed by the more pragmatic priorities of basic skill and examination-focused learning.

In short, little or no time or space is reserved in most British schools for the formal or focused education and/or development of character or virtue as such. Character education is therefore mostly left to chance, or — if thought about at all — assumed to be a by-product of other subjects or learning activities. Some schools seem to believe that good character is generally learned or picked up though the culture and ethos of the school, or perhaps more particularly developed or inspired though such whole-school activities as general assemblies or sporting events. Insofar, the need to find a particular space or time-slot for delivery of the Knightly Virtues programme in an already crowded school day, week or term was something of a problem for most schools. That said, the problem of finding a place for the programme was almost certainly less pressing in the primary context than it might have been in the secondary school in which examination pressure on the curriculum is especially intense and constraining. Moreover, the more 'progressive' climate or trend of British post-Plowden and Scottish 'Memorandum' primary education (see Plowden Report 1961, and Primary Memorandum 1965) towards more topic-based or integrated studies seems more accommodating to less standard or conventional curriculum input of the Knightly Virtues kind than more subject-centred secondary curricula. Despite this, however, primary school teachers are still under much contemporary pressure to teach the core skills of literacy and numeracy that are the staple and priority of official prescription. Hence, it was common for teachers who did successfully accommodate the Knightly Virtues programme to express regret that they were unable to spend more time on a programme in which they clearly recognized endless scope for broader educational development.

Literacy

Still, while the Knightly Virtues programme was from the outset liable to these general problems of curriculum accommodation, perhaps its strongest suit or advantage was the obvious vehicle it afforded for the promotion of general literacy. To be sure, while most teachers appreciated that this was not the main interest of the programme, they also recognized that it would be readily welcomed or 'sold' to head-teachers and other line managers as contributory or supplementary to education in general literacy. In this light, many teachers taught the programme as a replacement for their regular pupil literacy programme for five weeks, whilst others 'bolted' it onto the regular programme as a special project or topic taught sometimes for one afternoon a week. At all events, the four stories were relatively easily deployable as everyday occasions for literacy learning, either as read by teachers to pupils—who could then follow the reading in their own journals—or as reading by pupils on their own, or to each other, either in class or at home. In this regard, paired or partnered reading—with either peers or parents—was particularly encouraged. In the case of *The Merchant of Venice*, moreover, pupils were invited to act out sections of the play in small groups. In addition, those parts of the programme that required written responses from pupils provided yet further valuable opportunities for literacy learning. For example, having read and discussed the narrative of Gareth and Lynette, pupils were sometimes invited to compose their own short stories or poems about the courage or humility of Gareth.

In this connection, the opportunity that the programme offered for the learning of new vocabulary was particularly welcomed. Indeed, it appeared that many pupils had never actually heard or used the word 'virtue' as such before—though some had heard the phrase 'patience is a virtue' without really understanding what it meant. Likewise, while some of the virtues—such as love and courage—were fairly familiar to many pupils, others—such as humility and gratitude—appeared surprisingly unfamiliar or new. For example, when asked at the start of the programme to define humility, some pupils confused it with the word 'humiliation'. Hence, the learning of basic virtue vocabulary was a priority for the programme and one early journal activity simply invites pupils to try to define such key terms as 'character' and 'virtue' or to match virtue words to suggested definitions. To be sure, pupils learned much new vocabulary simply by attempting to read the stories—and this was also much assisted by deliberate retention of much of the language of the original literary works themselves. In this regard, it was gratifying, during feedback sessions, to hear pupils saying that although they had initially struggled with Shakespearian language, they had eventually managed to read (for example) *The Merchant of Venice* with a large measure of comprehension. Indeed, as already noted, the time-tested literary quality and value of the stories was regarded as an educationally sufficient—if not presently primary—reason for teaching them rather than as any sort of disadvantage or disincentive. As one primary 6 teacher wryly observed:

> When we looked at the text initially we thought 'oh my God, how are we going to do *The Merchant of Venice* with this lot?'—because we're ranging from a level 2 in Literacy all the way up to potentially 6. But actually the pupils really raised to the challenge and were better off for it.

Another common refrain of teacher feedback was precisely that the programme powerfully revived great stories from the past for pupils, many of whom had never heard of *Don Quixote,* or any of the stories of Shakespeare before. Indeed, teachers themselves were clearly pleased at and grateful for the opportunity to return to texts from their own youth or past schooling that had re-awakened their own enthusiasm for these tales. Thus, the general educational value of the Knightly Virtues stories for all and sundry seems nicely summed up by the remark of a primary 6 teacher: 'it's opened the world for them to read other stories and not be put off.'

Other Subjects

However, beyond such general primary literacy uses, the programme was also taught—with more explicit moral and character educational aims in view—within the context of such other subjects as PSHE, Citizenship, History, Art and Religious Education. Here, the fact that diverse aspects of the project met the criteria set for a wide range of primary subjects—and were therefore readily combined or interwoven in a cross-curricular way with other studies, themes and topics —proved to be highly attractive to teachers. In particular, however, the programme seemed to offer a novel entry point to the PSHE (Personal, Social and Health Education) curriculum—especially for addressing such generally controversial topics as 'how to live well' and 'how to live morally'. Again, since all four Knightly Virtues stories are set —albeit fictionally—in interesting periods of European history, they clearly offer much scope for exploration of past historical times and events of invaluable educational interest. Yet again, aside from already observed respects in which the programme is conducive to fostering literary expression, the Knightly Virtues project may be no less easily connected with other forms of creative and imaginative art. Thus, for example, the programme actually encourages pupils to design their own coats of arms, incorporating symbolic references to family, friends and other things of value and importance to them. This also invites invention of personal mottos that sum up their key moral values and aspirations — such as (in pupils' own words): *Never Give up* or *Live to Love*. Pupils are also encouraged to design cartoons picturing times when they sought to be virtuous — say honest or just — but found it difficult to be so.

That said, while the Knightly Virtues programme was fairly easily linked to or fitted in with other particular curriculum areas or subjects, many teachers liked it precisely because it could not be fitted into any one curriculum 'box' and usefully served to bring different subjects together in a more integrated or 'holistic' way. As one teacher observed: 'it is the combination of PSHE, character and literacy that made it special… although we would often start off with a discussion of literacy, we would end up talking about morals and character traits.' Pupils also clearly warmed to this aspect of the programme. As one primary 5 pupil remarked:

> In normal literacy lessons, you just read a book and they'll listen to you; and if you're good at reading you'll go and stuff that; but in this, you could learn from it and it was fun and you could relate to the characters and picture in your mind.

Teachers generally thought that programmes of the Knightly Virtues ilk were more than just simply another curriculum subject, and that they had an impact not only on the characters of pupils, but on the character, climate or ethos of the whole school. Thus, one teacher commented: 'this all goes hand in hand with our curriculum and our ethos in school that these sorts of things (virtues) are needed for a happy society.' Indeed, notwithstanding that the programme was designed for primary 5 and 6, some schools took the programme much further by adopting a whole school approach to some elements of it: for example, by encouraging pupils to present some of the stories in school assemblies. There were also occasions of primary 5 and 6 pupils reading the stories to younger pupils in the school, and many classes created wall displays based on the Knightly Virtues. The previously noted personal coats of arms of pupils would frequently be displayed on the corridor walls of schools and other displays focused on the eight knightly virtues were often hung up at school entrances.

The Knightly Virtues for Wider Contemporary Life

In addition to classroom and whole school activities, however, the programme has encouraged learning in, from and about contexts and issues of wider contemporary life. In this regard, the Knightly Virtues programme provides a convenient springboard for the exploration of further stories and issues of much modern or present day relevance. Thus, one of the activities of the programme invites classroom or homework research into some relatively recent historical figure who seems to have demonstrated one or more of the knightly virtues in his or her life or achievements — following which pupils are asked to report back on this research to their teacher and classmates. Among the particular characters insightfully researched by pupils in this way have been Florence Nightingale, Elizabeth Fry, Alexander Graham Bell and Mother Teresa. Of one such figure, a pupil wrote:

> Harriet Tubman is a great historical figure who showed service to others. Throughout her wild adventures she also showed love and humility to her family and also the slaves she rescued. Harriet also displayed self-discipline when her boss hit her with a rock. Harriet Tubman is someone I look up to as a role model as someone who stood her ground and fought for what she believed in. Harriet Tubman is an inspiration and someday I hope to inspire people and be as loving as Harriet Tubman. (Primary 6 girl)

Another pupil chose to write about his granddad as an historical figure as follows:

> I chose my granddad because he's quite old now but he went through World War II and this Other war in Yugo-slavia and he was one of the first, like, few people that came back to Kosovo. Even though it was still dangerous, they came back to help rebuild the country and he went through some very scary stuff. His stories still inspire me. (Primary 5 boy)

Yet another approach to exploring the contemporary implications or relevance of the Knightly Virtues focused on current news stories. Thus, one programme task encourages pupils to be on the look-out for recent significant news events — with particular regard to issues of social justice and moral honesty — and to create collages of headlines and images highlighting these. Among the news events that have featured in such collages have been Malala Yousafzai's courageous survival of the Taliban attack, stories of compensation for NHS whistle-blowers, and more local stories about (for example) the saving from closure of a neighbourhood library.

Piloting the Pack

The Knightly Virtues programme was piloted in its entirety in two primary schools — one in Birmingham and one in Derbyshire — and teaching sessions were fully observed in both schools by members of the development team. Following each pilot session, teachers and pupils were asked to comment on the content and presentation of lessons. Observations were recorded following each of the pilot sessions and feedback based on these was used in the finally developed version of the programme. Pupils also completed draft versions of the journals during the programme, and these were subsequently utilized in further development of the teaching pack and other supporting materials. Following the pilot, revisions were made to the text and this revision was sent to two experienced head-teachers for further review and feedback. On completion of this process, an illustrator was commissioned to design graphics for each of the stories to be used in the pupil journal. With these in place, the whole teaching pack was submitted for publication. The pack was then rolled out to schools across Britain that had expressed an interest in the programme. We may now turn in the next concluding chapter to some critical assessment of the apparent impact of the Knightly Virtues with regard to teaching or assisting pupils' understanding of moral character through stories.

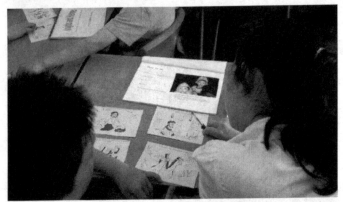

Chapter Seven

Knightly Virtues: Impact and Future Prospects

Prefatory Remarks

The case has been made in this work for retrieving great past narratives of cultural and literary inheritance for the education of moral character. The previous penultimate chapter of this work explored some issues of the practical delivery and implementation of the Knightly Virtues programme in British schools and this final chapter will close with some account of the responses of pupils, teachers and parents to the programme – with particular attention to its implications for parent–school partnership – and, drawing on these, with some suggestions for future developments. By March 2014, the Knightly Virtues programme had been undertaken by over 5,000 pupils from one hundred schools in England, Scotland and Wales. It has been well received in schools of all kinds, including faith and non-faith, state and private, and those in both urban and rural settings. It seems to have worked exceptionally well with the primary 5 and 6 pupils at which it was primarily targeted, although it also seems to have gone down well with the primary 4 pupils also exposed to the programme in some schools. The programme has also been subject to ongoing evaluation at almost every stage of its development and implementation. Regular interviews have been conducted with teachers, parents and pupils themselves, alongside continuous monitoring and analysis of work completed in pupil journals. All in all, this has generated a wealth of evidence regarding the impact of the programme—of which we may now attempt to give some flavour.

The evaluative reflections of this chapter will fall under three main headings. In the first place, we shall consider evidence to support the claim that the Knightly Virtues programme has succeeded in achieving one of its main aims of providing young people with the semantic building blocks of any basic comprehension of virtue or moral character in the form of enhanced knowledge or mastery of virtue words and concepts. Secondly, we shall consider some evidence that exposure to the Knightly Virtues stories has managed to go beyond simply helping pupils to understand better the language of virtue and character, by enabling them to apply it to their own personal moral character development—and, according to at least some sources, facilitating actual improvement of their moral attitudes and conduct. However, thirdly, we shall consider evidence (mainly) from parents that the Knightly Virtues programme has greatly helped to bridge the gap between home and school frequently addressed in educational policy-making as the issue or problem of home–school or teacher–parent 'partnership'.

The Semantic Building Blocks of Character

Previous research has indicated that contemporary youths are widely lacking an adequate vocabulary of character. In this regard, between 2007 and 2010, the British *Learning for Life* project (Arthur 2010) conducted a survey of almost 80,000 young people from ages 2 to 25 that seemed to show a marked level of unfamiliarity with if not actual ignorance of such basic moral terms as 'character' and 'virtue' among people of this age range. On this basis, it strongly recommended the revival or recovery of 'a language in which we can publicly discuss and personally appreciate human character'. This finding led David Lorimer (2014) of *Character Scotland* to observe:

> Given the finding that young people lack a common language of virtues and values and the fact that our culture encourages young people to turn outwards and neglect their inner lives, it is culturally vital to redress these imbalances. Character education has a significant role to play and engaging with the language of virtues and values is an excellent starting point.

It has therefore from the outset been a key aim of the Knightly Virtues programme to develop the knowledge and understanding of primary school pupils of the language of character and virtue, and tasks dedicated to this goal have featured conspicuously in the lesson plans and journal activities of the project. Further to this, however, the pro-gramme has also sought to press home to pupils that virtue terms are not 'stand-alone' or unrelated, but implicated in a complex web of moral discourse that calls for wider or more 'holistic' comprehension. As such, individual virtue terms are diagrammatically represented in the journal as parts of an interlocking system. So, while it is true that one early journal activity invites pupils to define virtues individually, they are asked hard on the heels of this to consider a wider range of virtues exhibited by the various characters in a given story and to rank these by order of their prominence in the narrative. Here, as it happens, while pupils differed somewhat in their virtue ratings and rankings of characters in individual stories, most seem to have regarded *love* and *humility* as overall highest virtues. At all events, the general aim of project and journal activities and exercises is to assist pupils to grasp not only how the eight key Knightly Virtues relate to each other, but also how they contribute to a larger integrated whole of moral character formation.

Thus, in the context of project evaluation, pupils were asked questions such as:

> We defined some virtue words earlier; have you used these words in conversation before?

and

> Can you give an example of when you have used the work since taking part on the programme?

From pupil responses to such questions, it seems clear that the Knightly Virtues programme did successfully promote acquisition of a new or at least extended and deepened virtue vocabulary. Thus, a primary 5 girl stated:

> By the time you finish Knightly Virtues, you will understand what justice means, what humility means, what self-discipline means; so you will be able to describe someone's character and they will be able to describe you.

Again, linking the Knightly Virtues programme explicitly to literacy, another primary 5 girl observed:

> I'm really happy that we did it because we learnt the virtues, and even after some of the words I got stuck on; but then I learnt them and then I moved up to a level 11 in reading because I've learnt more words.

Pupils also clearly appreciated the need for accurate use of virtue terms for understanding the development of moral character. For example a primary 5 pupil remarked that:

> The virtues help build character; it's important to know all of the virtues because they are like the life lessons.

However, pupil progress in learning about the relevance of virtue terms to understanding character was also clearly appreciated by teachers. In this regard, it was observed by one teacher that:

> The children really enjoyed finding out the eight specific virtues. They related to all — well most of them if not all — they stated their favourite ones, what they liked about the virtues.

relating to them. They wanted to write and they loved the journals and filling them in. It improved their literacy and writing because they felt they knew what to write and had something to write about. The boys really were exploring virtue—some more than others—but they were applying it.

However, it also seemed clear that the actual messages of the stories about the importance of cultivating good moral character were widely taken to heart—in, for example, the comments of many parents that the project had fuelled much interested home discussion about the character virtues exemplified by the various heroes and heroines of the stories.

Personal Character Formation

For it should by now be evident that the ultimate aspiration of the Knightly Virtues programme was not just to help pupils to come to clearer mastery of the vocabulary and/or language of virtue, but to foster or engage with some personal development of virtuous or moral character in the light of such greater clarity. To be sure, while it would be hard to prove empirically whether pupil conduct had actually improved for the better over the course of a few episodes of storytelling and questioning—even if this is the sort of development that is amenable to even longer term experimental testing—pupils were nevertheless encouraged throughout the programme to use the stories as vehicles for reflection on their own moral character strengths, weaknesses and aspirations. To this end, peer review of character qualities was encouraged as a stimulus to such critical self-evaluation. In one exercise, for example, pupils were precisely invited to think about how their classmates might regard them in terms of moral character. In another exercise, pupils were encouraged to reflect on the lives of those of their close acquaintance—such as parents, siblings or friends—with a view to the identification of morally exemplary attitudes or conduct. Such exercises seem to have been very effective in helping pupils to explore questions of who they are and who or what they might aspire to be in moral terms. To this end, the most protracted writing exercise of the project occurs at the end of the journal where pupils are invited to evaluate the whole programme and consider what they have learnt about themselves and their own characters from their engagement with it. It may be that the value and benefits of the Knightly Virtues programme are most strikingly apparent in the responses of pupils to this exercise. Thus, for example one primary 5 boy writes as follows:

> I think the Knightly Virtues project was great fun. It taught me more about myself and how the virtues are not just something you have; they make you who you are, they make you special. I have learned that virtues usually associated with knights can be shown by anyone.

In much the same spirit, another primary 5 boy writes:

> The programme has lots of messages and morals I can really relate to. I feel like all the stories have taught me a lesson about how to use the virtues. I have had to think about how I show the virtues and the one I think I display the most is love.

Indeed, pupils also sought to specify particular respects in which the programme had helped them to think about their personal conduct with a view to changing or modifying it. In this regard, a primary 5 girl offered an example of how she thought the programme had helped her to change her attitudes in a quite specific way:

> It has helped me calm down. Now we're getting older we're getting moody with our parents, and I was reading my book after I'd been up to my bed and I realised I needed to work on my discipline. So I went down and said sorry; so it helped me get over that I'd been rude to my mum and dad.

Another said, more simply, that: 'it has made me want to be a better person.'

However, other indications of the potentially transformative power of the Knightly Virtues programme seem evident from entries to pupil journals. As already noted, one activity invites pupils to represent or depict the frequent difficulty of telling the truth or owning up to misdemeanours in the form of cartoons. Responses to this exercise included that of a pupil who broke her mother's favourite flower-pot and owned up to it, another pupil who took chocolate from the cupboard when she was not supposed to and then told her father and another who admitted to her teacher that she had pushed over a friend. Despite the trivial nature of some of these episodes, we believe that they may be taken as real evidence of serious pupil reflection and deliberation on the considerable everyday difficulty of acting truthfully or honestly in the face of conflicting motivations — such as fear of punishment — of a morally significant kind. Indeed, if the heart of character development lies in the cultivation of capacities to deliberate with moral seriousness on cases of particular and personal moral concern, the cartoon exercise may be a very effective way of illustrating and/or personifying the abstract dilemmas of ethical theorizing in an enjoyable but nevertheless potentially character-formative way. With particular regard to the everyday moral challenge of honesty, a primary 5 girl observed:

> Like, if you're in a situation where at school for example you could lie and get out of trouble, or tell the truth and you get into trouble; like, it's really hard to decide with yourself, because, like, your head might be saying one thing and your heart another and then you have to be, like, brave and just, like, do the right thing and show honesty and take responsibility for what you've done.

To be sure, throughout the Knightly Virtues project, pupils are encouraged to apply the lessons of these old stories to their present-day lives and circumstances. To this end, one of the final activities of the programme invites pupils to identify an inspirational modern-day role model or 'local hero' who might fairly be held to exemplify one or more of the virtues of the key knightly virtues characters. While teachers, family members, local volunteers and friends featured fairly predictably among the many such exemplars identified by pupils, this task certainly seems to have served its intended purpose in bringing the virtues of the stories to contemporary life. However, many other approaches to personalizing or bringing to life the virtues were also tried: so, for example, rather than simply writing about (say) gratitude, pupils were also encouraged to illustrate the causes and objects of gratitude in their lives in the form of mind maps, flow charts and pictures.

Teaching the Complexities of Character: A School Case Study

Further to current evaluation of the effectiveness of Knightly Virtues stories in enhancing pupils' comprehension of both the language and conduct of virtue, it is here worth considering some of the responses of one particular school. Thus, the teachers at St Luke's Primary[1] offered two very distinctive reasons for regarding classic stories of the knightly virtues ilk as powerful vehicles for the exploration of complexities of moral character. First, they held that such stories provide an effective 'hook' for attracting the interest of young people. However, secondly, they thought that such stories focused very directly on the characters of their main protagonists, drawing immediate attention to issues of moral association and conduct. Here, with especially interesting reference to the affective or emotional aspects or components of moral or virtuous character, the head-teacher at St Luke's thought that over the years there had been some tendency to choose the 'wrong' stories for primary pupils:

> A while ago in this country we went down the wrong route where we tried to pretend to children that they didn't have bad emotions and that everything was sunny and rosy. This doesn't help because bad things do happen and we all have

---

[1]   http://www.st-lukes.derbyshire.sch.uk/

negative emotions. There isn't a person in this world that doesn't feel cross sometimes, doesn't feel resentful of a younger sibling, doesn't have emotions that we might call bad emotions. If we keep saying this, then a child could feel guilty because they have these emotions, they might think I have bad emotions and I'm naughty... but no, they're just human. Literature is a very good way to allow children to think about negative emotions. It enables children to understand they are not the only one that has ever felt angry and feeling angry is okay, but then what's not okay is to hurt someone because I am feeling angry. It's okay for me to be resentful that my parents have had a new baby but what's not okay is for me to be horrible to that baby. It's about what they do with the emotions and we work a lot with the children here to give them space to explore what might be considered bad feelings so they have the tools to handle those rather than just thinking negatively I'm a bad person.

In stories, as in real life, the right course of action is not always obvious or straightforward. The teachers at St Luke's claim that critical analysis of the decisions in this or that morally problematic circumstance of—for example—Don Quixote or Gareth helped their pupils to think about what might be the or an appropriate moral response. In reading the stories, pupils were encouraged to reflect on the complexity and often conflicted nature of human motives in morally challenging circumstances. In this regard, the Knightly Virtues stories seemed to provide an effective 'laboratory' for the study, cultivation and exercise of practical wisdom. In short, the teachers maintained that pupils actually learned lessons in practical deliberation and decision making from the stories and to apply them to their own lives.

That said, teachers also held that one advantage of using literature as a basis for reflection on issues of moral character and conduct is that it allowed for some personal detachment or distance. Such more detached or impersonal approach was said to be especially helpful in the case of pupils whose conduct was of a more challenging character, since it enabled them to appreciate the difference between good and bad decisions and conduct from a more objective or external perspective. As the head-teacher put it:

> Exploring negativity is of huge value. It helps children understand that they could have made a different choice that would have had a different outcome; and exploring it through literature shows children that they can make choices and see the consequences. Without the understanding of action and consequence we have a problem. This is often seen in children with special needs or chaotic households, or households of violence. They don't have the action–consequence connection and that is why they take part in risky behaviours. This will help people know how to work within a social group as adults; I can choose what I do and that will have consequences.

To be sure, the success of a project such as the Knightly Virtues programme — which is crucially aimed at stimulating capacities for independent and/or self-directed reflection on the nature of moral character and virtue — greatly depends on the right sort of delivery. Such delivery cannot be confined simply to reading the stories to pupils, or to direct instruction of their narrative content, and thought therefore needs to be given to developing teaching and learning styles conducive to the exercise of active moral and other reflection. A key task, in this regard, is to develop strategies that encourage or facilitate questioning and debate on the part of pupils. As the head-teacher of St Luke's says:

> The idea is that you as a teacher are a facilitator of learning and what you are doing is giving the children some knowledge, but also the means of exploring the knowledge; how you think creatively, how you work in groups and how you accept someone else's ideas of how we work. We know that this doesn't lend itself to all subjects, and unfortunately the new curriculum is even more about the need to just know facts. This is a great shame. I have done a lot of work about

creative thinking and enterprise and they are actually identical. They are saying the same thing. Industries want people who can work with each other and think of crazy ideas.

According to the head-teacher, if pupils are encouraged to engage with the meaning of what they are learning in an authentic or creative way, they are more likely to take the lessons of such learning to heart. To be sure, since the aim of the Knightly Virtues programme in particular and of any serious moral education in general can only be to give agents such authentic ownership over their moral deliberations and judgements, overly didactic teaching styles clearly have limited use—and it is with this in mind that the Knightly Virtues programme has generally sought to provide as much pupil-centred and interactive pedagogy as possible: for example, in the forms of small and whole group discussion as well as debates and role-play. At all events, given this general aim of the Knightly Virtues programme to cultivate pupils' knowledge and understanding, not only of virtue terms but of the complex logical grammar of moral reflection and deliberation, the head-teacher of St Luke's observed that:

> The children were given the language of the virtues and this really helped. I think the more words you have to describe feelings and emotions, the better. You then have the words to talk about what you are feeling, and it gives you the power to talk about it. It gave many different words to use that might resonate with someone. Words are wonderful and the more words we can give children the more we are going to help them through life. You won't develop your vocabulary, if you don't know what the word means. You won't grow and it's limiting potential.

In general, she observed that the impact of the programme had been felt throughout the whole school:

> When the older children did their assembly on the knightly virtues, the younger children got involved and the reception class were blown away by it and adopted it; so it changed

the teaching across school. Also, the children went to an event with other schools doing the Knightly Virtues project, and it was great to see all the children confident in what they were doing!

Knightly Virtues: Home and School Partnership

One recurring theme or refrain of latter day British educational policy-making has been that of 'partnership' between home and school. Whereas in the not too distant past schools often appeared to be impenetrable fortresses whose gates parents were strongly discouraged from crossing, this stand-off attitude of teachers to parents has certainly been eroded in recent educational policy and legislation — undoubtedly as one significant aspect of a general drift towards affirming the democratic rights of parents (to free choice to schooling and so on) as tax-paying 'consumers' with regard to the provision of such publicly funded services as school education. However, it has often seemed — perhaps particularly to professional teachers — that such attempts to give parents more of a voice in the education of their children has been something of a one-way street. In this regard, much official educational policy thinking and legislation regarding partnership seems to have been mostly concerned to spell out the obligations and duties of schools to provide full or fuller reports to parents of the educational or other progress of their offspring. So, for example, legislation in the wake of the *Parents Charter* (1994) and the White Paper *Excellence in Schools* (1997) has been largely concerned to ensure that schools provide parents with opportunities for consultation and information on the content of school provision including prospectuses and regular reports on pupil progress.

On the other hand, it seems fairly safe to say that official or informal efforts in the direction of developing more substantial forms of home–school or parent–teacher collaboration — or at least of home support for schooling (or vice versa) — have received less attention and been perhaps mainly confined to encouraging parents to assist with homework or to some voluntary parental help in classrooms. In this regard, to be sure, it may seem that one of the most important respects in which teachers and parents might usefully seek to work together—namely, on the education and formation of the moral values and character of young people—is also precisely one of the most sensitive and contentious. Indeed, insofar as it is widely held that parents have not just a responsibility but a right to be the primary architects of their children's characters, it is easy to see—especially in circumstances of potential tension or conflict between school and home values—why schools and teachers are often nervous about promoting beliefs or perspectives to which parents might object (as, for example, in cases where parents feel that a liberal or 'rationalist' education undermines their family religious values). From this viewpoint, the ideological and logistical prospects for cooperation or common purpose between home and school over something like education of moral values and character education may well seem more daunting than promising. While home–school cooperation on the teaching of literacy might appear feasible, such joint endeavour over the cultivation of moral values and character might well seem to go where angels fear to tread.

At the same time, while teachers, schools, educational and other public policy-makers might well fight shy of dictating how parents should bring up or form their children, it also seems widely assumed that some attention to the cultivation of pupils' moral values and character is also the responsibility of schools. In this regard, the previously noted response to the *Populus* poll finding that parents actually do think that schools can and should teach character education might well seem to schools and teachers not only another case of parents 'passing the buck', but of wanting to have their cake and eat it too. It seems that schools are expected to fill the gap left by inadequate or defective parenting; but when they try seriously to do this, parents complain that schools are going where they have no business. From this point of *impasse*, however, it might seem that the only remaining viable option is some serious practical cooperation between schools and parents over the business of helping young people to acquire sound moral values and form good moral character. In this regard, the distinguished character educator Thomas Lickona has observed: 'schools that reach out to families and include them in character-building efforts greatly enhance their chances for success with students' (Lickona 1996). Insofar, while one might continue to insist that parents are — or should be — the primary agents of moral and character formation, schools and teachers might well be useful allies in this role. Indeed, such alliance would appear crucial to the success of either effective schooling or parenting; for there is surely small hope of nurturing such virtues as honesty, compassion and courage in schools if these are to be neglected in the home — or of course vice versa. Still, it might now be asked how one might even begin to go about developing or promoting cooperation or rapprochement in such a weighty business as moral education and character formation in schools.

Here, while one could not reasonably expect such a small-scale project as the Knightly Virtues programme to provide anything like a final solution to this large issue, it can claim some limited but significant success in having brought schools and homes, teachers and parents, together in addressing serious questions of human moral life and association. As already noticed, parents were invited and encouraged throughout the Knightly Virtues programme to share or contribute to the learning experiences of their children. Since pupils were allowed to take their journals home, parents were able to read the stories with their sons and daughters as well as to take a fairly active role in the completion of some journal activities and exercises. Indeed, parents were actually asked to offer some comment — in the form of journal entries — both during and at the conclusion of the programme. Again, as in the case of teachers, many parents seemed pleased that their sons and daughters were encountering some of the same stories that they had read at school and they commended the programme for stimulating rich home conversations about the moral import of these narratives. In this vein, one parent observed: 'he comes home from school and explains a lot about the virtues. It has also ignited his interest in Shakespeare—which pleases me greatly as I am a Shakespeare fan.' Pupils themselves were also clearly touched by such parental approval and enthusiasm for the programme. As one primary 6 girl stated:

> My parents, especially my mum, she thought that it was something different for us to learn at school. It wasn't something that we learned all the time and it was something that really made us think about our character and how it's important to show good virtues and personalities in life, because it's important to be a good person.

Again, despite previously noted difficulties about the prospect of any very reliable or accurate monitoring or tracking of actual (behavioural) moral improvement—especially over the short period of the Knightly Virtues programme—many parents did nevertheless claim to have discerned some progress in the quality of their children's moral reflection and attitudes. Thus, one parent observed: 'I believe the project has helped Amy become more self-aware and to figure out how our virtues and personal qualities make us who we are'; and another that: 'William has learned to think a little more deeply about qualities we might take for granted, such as gratitude, honesty and service. He has been surprised by some of his thoughts.' And some did even go the extra mile in claming that the programme had improved the actual moral conduct of their children; thus: 'Alicia has learnt a lot about character and different virtues as she is displaying the virtues more.' Certainly many noticed a positive impact on literacy; in the words of one parent: 'Sam has really enjoyed this so far. He has come home full of enthusiasm and wanting to extend his reading he has done as part of the project.' All in all, however, the apparently overwhelming parental approval of the project might well be summed up by the parent who commented: 'I think this is a well thought out project which is thought provoking and captures the children's imagination.'

So while we are far from claiming that the Knightly Virtues project has solved all major contemporary problems of how to teach sound moral values and form good moral character in school or home—or of securing the required level of cooperation and partnership of teachers and parents in this weighty task—it may with some justification be claimed that it has at least brought teachers and parents together in a spirit of well nigh unanimous enthusiasm for joint reflection, deliberation and debate on profound educationally relevant questions of how as humans we might or should morally live.

Where Might the Knightly Virtues Go Next?

However, while the success of the Knightly Virtues programme has been encouraging, nothing in this world is ever finished or perfect and there is clearly scope for reflection on how school projects of this broad moral and character educational kind might be refined or improved for future deployment. In this regard, directly inspired by the Knightly Virtues project, other more or less similar story-based character education ventures are presently under construction in Britain and elsewhere. So, for example, Jon Davison—himself one of the original architects of the Knightly Virtues programme—is developing a whole series of additional stories, together with a teaching pack along broadly similar lines to the parent project of present concern. The first story, that of the American civil rights heroine Rosa Parks, has already been completed and is currently in use in schools. This has not only served to bring the life and personal virtues of an important modern day heroine to the attention of British primary pupils, but has also occasioned rich educational exploration of an important event of modern history in which issues of political and social justice and fairness are conspicuously implicated. Indeed, this story has already been widely used by schools during Black History month. Professor Davison is also developing a further ten stories — or 'clusters' of stories — with accompanying resources, materials and lesson plans. These include narratives of Beowulf, Robin Hood, Sir Gawain (and the Green Knight), Joan of Arc and Anne Frank. True to the spirit of the original Knightly Virtues programme, Davison's 'extension' project aims at an inspirational mix of moral heroes and heroines from history, legend and myth. The main novelty of this programme is to group the stories into 'clusters' that might then be taught under various thematic headings, thereby enabling further flexible accommodation to prescribed school curricula. One such cluster under current construction is that of *Fables, Myths and Legends,* which draws on stories from Greek, Roman, Norse and other myths and legends, as well as from the fables of Aesop and others. Another addresses the theme of *Women of Courage,* drawing on stories of more or less past heroines and reformers such as Emmeline Pankhurst, Amy Johnson, Pocahontas, Lucy Stone, Mary Seacole, Florence Nightingale, Harriet Tubman, Annie Oakley and Maria Montessori. However, another quite separate narrative based programme — also broadly inspired by the Knightly Virtues project — is currently being developed by Jen Lexmond under the heading of *Fairy Stories.* As the heading indicates, this aims to explore the present day moral relevance of a range of suitably adapted or re-worked classical fairytales. A distinguishing feature of this project is its explicit involvement of young people themselves in the creation and development of both stories and learning materials. This programme also specifically aims to explore the historically and culturally conditioned gender assumptions of such classical stories, myths and legends with a view to promoting deeper understanding of how these have shaped — and continue to shape — the self-images and character development of boys and girls of today.

Teaching Character Through Stories

We hope that this chapter has shown that whatever its limitations and/or shortcomings, the Knightly Virtues project—and the programme developed to deliver it in schools—does seem to have been well received by pupils, teachers and parents alike. Hence, in these final remarks, it is right and proper to express our very deep appreciation of the extraordinarily generous and enthusiastic response of all pupils, teachers and parents who participated in this project, whose commitment and hard work has greatly contributed to its success. That said, we can also think of no better way of concluding this work than with some appreciation and celebration of the project stories and their authors themselves—which were clearly the real key to the success of this project. For if anything has become clear from this venture it is surely the compelling and enduring power of tales of the Knightly Virtues variety themselves—which have lately proved no less a source of delight and edification to the architects of this project than to those to whom it was delivered.

For far from being seen as outdated and irrelevant by contemporary pupils—and/or teachers and parents—the Knightly Virtues stories were clearly perceived as sources of powerful insight into some of the most basic and enduring features, issues and problems of the human moral condition. While the stories were quite new to many pupils, it seems that they were able to relate to or identify with them with an immediacy that belied any suggestion of out-datedness. From this viewpoint, it should hardly need saying, it is depth and insight that makes for a great story rather than latest fashion. Some pupils even remarked that the stories were *better* and/or *held more meaning* than more recent stories they read in schools or at home. This seems to have frequently surprised teachers who subsequently confessed some pre-programme apprehension that the stories would be 'lost' on their pupils or generally beyond their comprehension. However, such doubts were soon allayed by pupil reactions to the stories on the day—of which the following can be taken as fairly typical:

> Some books are made to make people happy; they don't really have a meaning, there's no morals. In these older stories, we're having fun reading them but they also teach you something.

In our view, such comments contribute in their albeit small way to a larger educational case for the inclusion of classic stories such as those of Knightly Virtues—not only for their insight into moral association and character but for their inherent human, cultural, spiritual, artistic and aesthetic value—in the curricula of contemporary state and other schools. Insofar, our last and most significant tribute must go to the creators of the Knightly Virtues stories—and of other literature of tried and tested human and cultural value—whose works have continued to give pleasure to countless generations as well as stimulating the reflection of young and old alike on the deepest and most serious questions of human moral life and character.

References

Annas, J. (2011) *Intelligent Virtue,* Oxford: Oxford University Press.

Anscombe, G.E.M. (1981) 'Modern moral philosophy', in Anscombe, G.E.M., *The Collected Philosophical Papers of G.E.M. Anscombe: Volume III Ethics, Religion and Politics,* Oxford: Basil Blackwell.

Aristotle (1941a) *Nicomachean Ethics,* in McKeon, R. (ed.) *The Basic Works of Aristotle,* New York: Random House.

Aristotle (1941b) *Poetics,* in McKeon, R. (ed.) *The Basic Works of Aristotle,* New York: Random House.

Arthur, J. (2003) *Education and Character: The Moral Economy of Schooling,* London: Routledge/Falmer.

Arthur, J. (2010) *Of Good Character: Exploration of Virtues and Values in 3–25 Year Olds,* Exeter: Imprint Academic.

Arthur, J. and Harrison, T. (2014) *Schools of Character,* Birmingham: Jubilee Centre for Character and Virtues, accessed from http://issuu.com/careerstudio/docs/jubilee_centre_-_schools_of_charact

Bedford, E. (1956-57) 'Emotions', *Proceedings of the Aristotelian Society,* 57, 283–304.

Birdwell, J. and Millar, C. (2013) *Service Generation,* London: Demos.

Bohlin, K. (2005) *Teaching Character Education through Literature,* London and New York: Routledge/Falmer.

Boormnan, J. (1981) *Excalibur,* [Movie], Orien Pictures.

Burrow, J.A. (ed.) (1972) *Sir Gawaine and the Green Knight,* Harmondsworth: Penguin.

Carr, D. (2003b) 'Character and moral choice in the cultivation of virtue', *Philosophy,* 78, 219–232.

Carr, D. (2007) 'Religious education, religious literacy and common schooling: A philosophy and history of skewed reflection', *Journal of Philosophy of Education*, 41 (4), 659–673.

Cervantes, M. (1998) *Don Quixote*, Ware: Wordsworth Classics of Great Literature.

Dancy, J. (2004) *Ethics without Principles*, Oxford: Oxford University Press.

Dent, N.J.H. (1984) *The Moral Psychology of the Virtues*, Cambridge: Cambridge University Press.

Department for Education (1991) *Parents Charter*, London: HMSO.

De Sousa, R. (1987) *The Rationality of Emotion*, Cambridge, MA: MIT Press.

Dickens, C. (2001) *Hard Times*, London: Dover Publications.

Fletcher, R. (1989) *The Quest for El Cid*, Oxford: Oxford University Press.

Foot, P. (1978) *Virtues and Vices*, Oxford: Blackwell.

Geach, P.T. (1977) *The Virtues*, Cambridge: Cambridge University Press.

Gies, F. (1984) *The Knight in History*, London: Robert Hale.

Gilligan, C. (1982) *In a Different Voice: Psychological Theory and Women's Development*, Cambridge, MA: Harvard University Press.

Hare, R.M. (1952) *The Language of Morals*, Oxford: Oxford University Press.

Hallberg, F. (1987) 'Journal writing as person making', in Fulwiler, T. (ed.) *The Journal Book*, Portsmouth, NH: Heinemann.

Hartshorne, H. and May, M.A. (1928) *Studies in the Nature of Character*, New York: Macmillan.

Hirst, P.H. (1974) *Moral Education in a Secular Society*, London: London University Press.

Hobbes, T. (1968) *Leviathan*, Penguin: Harmondsworth.

Hooker, B. and Little, M.O. (eds.) (2001) *Moral Particularism*, Oxford: Oxford University Press.

Hume, D. (1969) *A Treatise of Human Nature*, Harmondsworth: Penguin.

Hursthouse, R. (1999) *On Virtue Ethics*, Oxford: Oxford University Press.

Jacobs, J. (2001) *Choosing Character*, Ithaca, NY: Cornell University Press.

Jubilee Centre for Character and Virtues (2013) *A Framework for Character Education*, Birmingham: Jubilee Centre for Character and Virtues, accessed from http://www.jubileecentre.ac.uk/472/character-education/the-framework

Kant, I. (1967) *The Critique of Practical Reasoning and Other Works on the Theory of Ethics*, Abbott, T.K. (trans.), London: Longmans.

Kenny, A. (1963) *Action, Emotion and Will*, London: Routledge and Kegan Paul.

Kohlberg, L. (1984) *Essays on Moral Development: Volume I*, New York: Harper Row.

Kristjánsson, K. (2007) *Aristotle, Emotions and Education*, Aldershot: Ashgate.

Kristjánsson, K. (2013) 'Ten myths about character, virtue and virtue education—and three well-founded misgivings', *British Journal of Educational Studies*, 61 (3), 269–287.

Lapsley, D.K. and Power, F.C. (eds.) (2005) *Character Psychology and Character Education*, Notre Dame, IN: University of Notre Dame Press.

Lexmond, J. and Grist, M. (eds.) (2010) *The Character Enquiry*, London: Demos.

Lickona, T. (1992) *Educating for Character: How Our Schools Can Teach Respect and Responsibility*, New York: Bantam Books.

Lickona. T. (1996) 'Eleven principles of effective character education', *Journal of Moral Education*, 25 (1), 93–100.

Lockwood, A. (2009) *The Case for Character Education: A Developmental Approach*, New York: Teacher College Press.

Lorimer, D. (2014) *Articulating a Language of Character*. Birmingham: Jubilee Centre, accessed from http://www.jubileecentre.ac.uk/464/character-education/research

Mace, C.A. & Peters, R.S. (1961–62) 'Emotions and the category of passivity', *Proceedings of the Aristotelian Society*, 62, 117–142.

MacIntyre, A.C. (1981) *After Virtue*, Notre Dame. IN: Notre Dame Press.

MacIntyre, A.C. (1988) *Whose Justice, Which Rationality?*, Notre Dame, IN: Notre Dame Press.

MacIntyre, A.C. (1992) *Three Rival Versions of Moral Enquiry*, Notre Dame, IN: Notre Dame Press.

MacIntyre, A.C. (1999) 'How to appear virtuous without actually being so', in Halstead, J.M. and McLaughlin, T.H. (eds.) *Education in Morality*, London, Routledge.

Malory, Sir T. (1986) *Le Morte D'Arthur*, London: Omega Books.

Mann, A. (1961) *El Cid* [Movie], Allied Pictures.

Noddings, N. (1983) *Caring: A Feminist Approach to Ethics*, Berkeley, CA: University of California Press.

Nussbaum, M. (1988) 'Non-relative virtues: An Aristotelian approach', in Nussbaum, M.C. and Sen, A. (eds.) (1993) *The Quality of Life*, Oxford: Oxford University Press.

Nussbaum, M. (1995) 'Aristotle on human nature and the foundations of ethics', in Altham, J.E.J. and Harrison, R. (eds.) *World, Mind and Ethics*, Cambridge: Cambridge University Press.

Nussbaum, M.C. (1997) 'Emotions as judgements of value and importance', in Bilimoria, P. & Mohanty, J.N. (eds.) *Relativism, Suffering and Beyond: Essays in Memory of Bimal K. Matilal*, Oxford: Oxford University Press.

Peters, R.S. (1966) *Ethics and Education*, London: George Allen and Unwin.

Peters, R.S. (1972a) 'Reason and passion', in Dearden, R.F., Hirst, P.H. and Peters, R.S. (eds.) *Education and the Development of Reason*, London: Routledge & Kegan Paul.

Peters, R.S. (1972b) 'The education of the emotions', in Dearden, R.F., Hirst, P.H. and Peters, R.S. (eds.) *Education and the Development of Reason*, London, Routledge and Kegan Paul.

Peters, R.S. (1981) *Moral Education and Moral Development*, London: George Allen and Unwin.

Plato (1961) *Gorgias*, in Hamilton, E. and Cairns, H. (eds.) *Plato: The Collected Dialogues*, Princeton, NJ: Princeton University Press.

Plowden Report (1967) *Children and their Primary Schools*, London: HMSO.

Popper, K.R. (2002) *The Logic of Scientific Discovery*, London: Routledge Classics.

Primary Memorandum (1966) *Primary Education in Scotland*, Scottish Education Department, Edinburgh: HMSO.

Rawls, J. (1999) *A Theory of Justice*, Cambridge, MA: Harvard University Press.

Rousseau, J.-J. (1973) *The Social Contract and Other Discourses*, London: Dent.

Ryan, K. (1995) 'The ten commandments of character education', *School Administrator*, September.

Ryan, K. and Bohlin, K. (1999) *Building Character in Schools: Practical Ways to Bring Moral Instruction to Life*, San Francisco, CA: Jossey-Bass.

Santayana, G. (1968) 'Tragic philosophy', in Henfrey, N. (ed.) *Selected Critical Writings of George Santayana*, Cambridge: Cambridge University Press.

Scheffler, I. (1983) *The Language of Education,* Springfield, IL: Charles C. Thomas.

Seldon, A. (2013) *Why the Development of Character is More Important than Exam Results in Schools,* Birmingham: Jubilee Centre for Character and Virtues, accessed from http://www.jubileecentre.ac.uk/464/character-education/research.

Shakespeare, W. (1971) *Hamlet*, Cambridge: Cambridge University Press.

Shakespeare, W. (2005) *The Merchant of Venice*, London: Penguin Shakespeare Series.

Simon, S.B., Howe, L.W. and Kirschenbaum, H. (1972) *Values Clarification: A Handbook of Strategies for Teachers and Students*, New York: Hart.

Solomon, R. (1983) *The Passions: The Myth and Nature of Human Emotion*, Notre Dame, IN: Notre Dame Press.

Solomon, R. (1988) 'On emotions as judgements', *American Philosophical Quarterly*, 25, 183–191.

Taylor, M. (1975) *Progress and Problems in Moral Education,* Slough: NFER Publishing.

Taylor, C. (1989) *Sources of the Self: The Making of the Modern Identity*, Cambridge: Cambridge University Press.

Tennyson, A. (1989) *Idylls of the King*, Harmondsworth: Penguin Classics.

White Paper (1997) *Excellence in Schools*, London: HMSO

Wilson, J. (1990) *A New Introduction to Moral Education*, London: Cassell.

Index

BOOST SELF-ESTEEM

Honor Head

W

FRANKLIN WATTS
LONDON•SYDNEY

Published in paperback in Great Britain in 2020
by The Watts Publishing Group
© The Watts Publishing Group 2020

Managing editor: Victoria Brooker
Design: Sophie Burdess

Image Credits: Shutterstock – all images Good Studio
apart from Iveta Angelova & Ollikeballoon
graphic elements throughout;
LOLE 20l, ONYX 21 tc, Zarian 7c.

ISBN: 978 1 4451 7060 2 (hbk)
ISBN: 978 1 4451 7061 9 (pbk)

Printed in China

FSC
www.fsc.org
MIX
Paper from
responsible sources
FSC® C104740

Franklin Watts
An imprint of
Hachette Children's Group
Part of the Watts Publishing Group
Carmelite House
50 Victoria Embankment
London EC4Y 0DZ
An Hachette UK Company
www.hachette.co.uk
www.franklinwatts.co.uk

CONTENTS

WHAT IS SELF-ESTEEM?

Self-esteem is what you think about yourself
and how much you like who you are.

GOOD OR HIGH SELF-ESTEEM...

That looks scary but I'll give it a try.

I can score this!

I failed last time, but I will pass this time.

I worked so hard for this. I am proud of myself!

I know everyone has new trainers, but I like my old ones.

Wow, my hair looks great today!

Bad or low self-esteem ...

You can change your self-esteem
and the way you think about yourself.
Just by opening this book you've made a start!

Well done!

1. BELIEVE YOU ARE SPECIAL

Believing you are special is not about thinking you should have all the attention and everyone running around after you. It is about accepting that you are you, faults and all, and believing that you deserve to be successful and happy.

JOIN IN THE CONVERSATION – YOU HAVE SOMETHING VALUABLE TO SAY

LEARN FROM YOUR MISTAKES AND MOVE ON

LOOK FORWARD TO TRYING AGAIN

LIKE WHO YOU ARE

Be proud of how you look, how you think, what you wear and who your friends are. Be yourself.

Set your own goals. These can be short-term goals...

SWIM A LENGTH OF THE POOL

STUDY FOR MY MATHS EXAM

LEARN THAT NEW DANCE

LEARN TO KNIT

FINISH MY BOOK

GO FOR A WALK EVERY DAY

... or goals for the future.

HEART SURGEON

OLYMPIC ATHLETE

BEST-SELLING AUTHOR

BUSINESS OWNER

GAMES DEVELOPER

STAR VLOGGER

DREAM YOUR OWN DREAM

BE AWESOME!

BE BOLD!

GO FOR IT, AS LONG AS IT IS WHAT YOU TRULY WANT!

DO WHAT YOU LOVE

2. BE BODY POSITIVE

WHAT DO YOU SEE WHEN YOU LOOK IN THE MIRROR?

Poor body image is caused by lots of things, especially film stars and vloggers who look glamorous all the time. They make 'perfection' seem like the ideal and that can make others feel inferior. But underneath the make-up and the clothes, they're the same as all of us.

REMEMBER, WHATEVER YOU LOOK LIKE, EVERYONE HAS SOMETHING SPECIAL ABOUT THEM TO FEEL PROUD ABOUT.

SELF-IMAGE IS NOT JUST ABOUT HOW YOU LOOK ON THE OUTSIDE, IT'S ABOUT WHO YOU ARE INSIDE...

3. GET HEALTHY

A healthy lifestyle helps to keep us physically and mentally fit.
Your body is amazing. It is strong and powerful. Be proud of your body.

Exercise not only keeps you fit, it makes you feel good.
When you do exercises that make your heart beat faster,
your body releases chemicals that make you feel happy.
Even washing the car, going for a walk or tidying your room
(yes, really) can give you a sense of having achieved something.

MAKE YOUR HEART PUMP FASTER TO STAY FIT

STRETCH OUT TO BUILD STRENGTH AND STAY SUPPLE

Worried about your weight? See a doctor who can give you advice about how to get healthy.

Did you know that food can affect our emotions and thinking?
Too much fast food, ready-made meals, sugar and fried food
can make us tired, grumpy, thick-headed and feel down
about ourselves and the world.

Eat great, think great

Feel sluggish, think sluggish

Super sleep

After all that good food and exercise
you will probably sleep better, too. Getting
a good night's sleep can make you feel
more positive about yourself.

4. CHANGE YOUR THINKING

A quick switch in how you think can boost your self-esteem.
These examples show easy ways you can change the way you think.

That was a great test paper, well done, but question D was not quite right.

I am so useless at science.

WHAT'S WRONG WITH MARY'S THINKING?

She is filtering out the good things her teacher said and only hearing the negative comments.

QUICK SWITCH:

I'm pleased I did well. I'll do some research into question D for next time.

Ahmed hasn't rung me back, I must have done something wrong.

WHAT'S WRONG WITH FRED'S THINKING?

People with low self-esteem always think everything is their fault even though there is no reason to think this.

QUICK SWITCH:

I hope Ahmed is okay. I haven't heard from him. I'll go round and see him.

Instead of talking down your achievements, be proud of them, no matter how small they are.

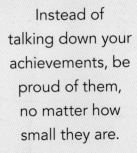

I only got top marks because the questions were so easy.

QUICK SWITCH:

Great, top marks! All that revision paid off.

No point in asking to join in, they won't want me.

Is the boy a mind reader? I don't think so! Because of low self-esteem he is assuming the others won't want to let him join them.

QUICK SWITCH:

That looks fun. I'll see if they want an extra player.

I am so useless at this. I'll never play again.

People with high self-esteem realise that they need to practise to get better instead of thinking they are no good at something.

QUICK SWITCH:

Hmm, looks like I need a bit more practice before the next time!

13

5. BE POSITIVE

Positive words and thoughts can help you behave in a more positive way. Take time to look in the mirror and say positive things to yourself. These are called affirmations.

I AM KIND AND CARING.

I WILL GET BETTER AT THIS.

I AM PROUD OF ME.

I AM CREATIVE.

I AM FUN TO BE WITH.

I HELP PEOPLE.

I WILL ACHIEVE ANYTHING I WANT.

Whatever the situation, if you have negative thoughts or words, replace them with something positive.

I CAN DO THIS.

I CAN SUCCEED.

I AM AN IMPORTANT TEAM MEMBER.

I AM STRONG.

I WILL TRY NEW THINGS.

I AM A GREAT PERSON TO HAVE AS A FRIEND.

I LOVE BEING ME.

6. CHANGE YOUR BEHAVIOUR

Part of improving our self-esteem is to behave in a positive way. Try and turn negative behaviour into positive behaviour. It may be hard at first, but it will get easier.

My friend really upset me, but I don't want to make a fuss.

Any decision I make is bound to be wrong.

You really upset me. Can we talk about it?

I've decided what I want to do.

No point in bothering to revise. I'm going to fail anyway.

I'm going to do my best in the exams, so I'd better get revising.

Strong, positive body language will help you to behave in a more positive way.

Make eye contact. This shows you are interested and confident.

Sit and stand up straight. Good posture will help your breathing and make you feel more confident.

Smile at people! It will make you feel better as well.

Take deep breaths before you enter a room or start a conversation, to calm your mind.

Don't fidget, tap your fingers or feet, shuffle or look around all the time. Try and keep your hands, feet and body relaxed.

7. BE ASSERTIVE

Being assertive is not the same as being aggressive,
rude, nasty or demanding.

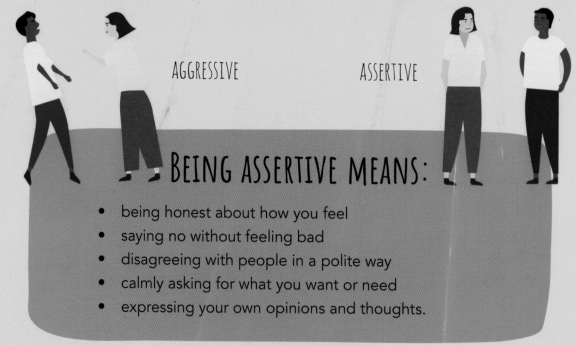

AGGRESSIVE

ASSERTIVE

BEING ASSERTIVE MEANS:

- being honest about how you feel
- saying no without feeling bad
- disagreeing with people in a polite way
- calmly asking for what you want or need
- expressing your own opinions and thoughts.

DON'T BE PASSIVE

If you feel that you always have to please others and ignore
your own feelings and wishes, you could end up...

FRUSTRATED

ANGRY

RESENTFUL

HATING
YOURSELF

Think before you speak

Practise 'I' and 'My'

I feel...

I'd like...

My favourite is...

I'd prefer...

My choice is...

Your wishes and opinions matter as much as anyone else's.

8. BE CONFIDENT

Being confident is about how you feel about yourself and your abilities. Increasing self-confidence builds up self-esteem.

Ways to boost self-confidence...

Learning something new helps to boost self-esteem. If you try something and it doesn't work, it may not be for you. Have a go at something else, but never stop trying!

DON'T COMPARE YOURSELF TO OTHERS

We all have different skills and abilities, likes and dislikes.
Don't be embarrassed to be yourself.

When you feel afraid of trying something new,
channel that fear into energy to help you do your best.
Be your own superhero!

9. DON'T FEAR FAILURE

Low self-esteem can often lead to a fear of failure.
This causes problems such as:

ANXIETY

FEELING SICK

FEAR

SLEEPLESS NIGHTS

STRESS

NOT EATING

PANIC

I'm finishing my revision for the exam tonight.

I'm not going to bother. I know I'll fail.

If I don't get top marks, it will be a disaster.

I was going to try that new sport's club, but I'll do it another time.

WHICH PERSON HERE HAS FEAR OF FAILURE?

WAIT! FAILING IS GOOD FOR YOU!

Really?

Failing and trying again builds up your confidence.

Failing makes you realise people love you and want to be with you for who you are, not what you've achieved.

When you fail, you try again and get better and better.

Failing gives you courage to try new things.

Break out of your comfort zone!

Our comfort zone is the space where we feel comfortable with people and situations we know. Breaking free of your comfort zone means you have more fun, are more interesting and won't get bored!

COMFORT ZONE

Be brave, take a risk.
That is what makes life exciting!

10. CONTROL YOUR SOCIAL MEDIA

Social media use can cause low self-esteem.
But how?

Others seem to be having a better time, making us feel boring and dull

Glamorous people making us feel that we are not good enough

FOMO (fear of missing out) is thinking that if we are not available all the time we will lose friends and miss out

Making us feel worthless if we don't get enough likes

Cyberbullying making us feel scared and alone

THESE ARE ALL POSSIBLE SCREEN-DEMONS THAT CAN MAKE US FEEL LOW.

IF YOUR SOCIAL MEDIA LIFE MAKES YOU FEEL LIKE ANY OF THESE THEN…

... STOP! Take Control!

Enjoy the life you have.

Spend face-to-face time with friends and family.

Try new hobbies and clubs.

Have digital-free times – it can be an hour twice a day, then try a whole day and what about a whole week?

Focus on the positive, being strong and healthy, having a supportive family and good friends.

Block bullies and report cyberbullying to a trusted adult, your school or the police.

Look for vloggers who make you feel good about yourself or have a shared interest.

SHOW THE SCREEN WHO'S IN CHARGE!

11. BUILD UP
YOUR LIFE SKILLS

Building life skills will develop strong self-esteem.
Relationship skills help you to build supportive friendships.

Accept not
everyone will want
to be your friend.

Don't judge
other people.

Be a good
listener.

Realise other
people are scared
or nervous, too.

Learn to laugh
at yourself.

Be kind
and honest.

Accept not
everyone will agree
with you.

Don't be nasty
to others, online
or face-to-face.

Accept others'
mistakes as well
as your own.

Be loyal.

COPING SKILLS WILL HELP YOU WHEN LIFE GETS TOUGH.

Feeling anxious about something? Visualise it going well. Take a few minutes to close your eyes and see yourself succeeding. Believe you can do it. Then take a deep breath and go!

Feeling stressed? Find somewhere quiet, close your eyes, slowly breathe in through your nose and out through your mouth until you feel calmer.

Write down your worries and fears... they can look less scary on paper.

Learn to talk to someone when things get tough – a friend, family member, online forum or helpline.

12. BE KIND TO YOURSELF

Always putting yourself down? Take some time out to think about how wonderful you really are.

WRITE DOWN 5 THINGS...

☑ … you really like about yourself

☑ … you like about your appearance

☑ … that make you feel happy

☑ … you would like to achieve in the next year

☑ … that make you proud of yourself

THAT'S LOADS OF THINGS THAT ARE REALLY COOL ABOUT YOU!

My Book of Me

Write out a list of the things you are good at and anything that makes you happy. Look at this when you feel you can't do anything right. Add something new to your book every day.

I make people laugh.

I make the best cheese sandwiches.

I can tap dance.

My cat loves me!

I love my cat!

I am great at spelling.

I am learning to cook.

I am patient.

I love listening to music.

I visit granny every week.

I am loyal to my friends.

I always help with the housework.

I work hard at school.

I scored the best goal of the season.

I AM SPECIAL ... I AM ME!

WHERE TO GET HELP

Talk to your carers, a trusted adult, a teacher or your friends
about how you feel. If there is no one you want to talk to,
there are loads of places online that can help you.

Chat rooms and forums are great for talking to people who
feel the same way as you do and may have had similar experiences.
However never share personal details with anyone, no matter
how genuine they seem. And never meet up with strangers.
Telephone helplines are places where you can talk to someone
who is specially trained to understand what you are going through.
They won't judge you or make you do anything you don't want to do.
You don't have to be embarassed or ashamed or silly
about what you tell them. They will be understanding, kind and supportive.

www.childline.org.uk/info-advice/your-feelings/mental-health
Message or call the 24 hour helpline
for advice or someone who'll just listen.
The helpline is 0800 1111

https://papyrus-uk.org
A place to go if you have thoughts
about harming yourself or suicide.
HopelineUK 0800 068 41 41

www.samaritans.org
A place where anyone can go
for advice and comfort.
The helpline is 08457 90 90 90

www.sane.org/get-help
Help and support for anyone affected
by mental and emotional issues.
The helpline is 0300 304 7000

www.gosh.nhs.uk/children/general-health-advice/eat-smart
How to eat for a better, healthier diet.

https://kidshealth.org/en/kids/self-esteem.html
Tips on how to build your self-esteem.

www.supportline.org.uk
A charity giving emotional support to young people.
The helpline is 01708 765200

kidshealth.org/en/kids/feeling
Advice on managing emotions.

www.youngminds.org.uk
Advice for young people
experiencing bullying, stress
and mental or emotional anxieties.

www.brainline.org/article/who-me-self-esteem-people-disabilities
How to boost self-esteem regardless of disabilities.

SHOUT!
A text-only 24/7 helpline for anyone suffering from
emotional and mental issues or going through a crisis.
Text 85258 and a trained volunteer will be there to help.

Or settle down with a book...

**You Are Awesome: Find Your Confidence
and Dare to be Brilliant at (Almost) Anything**
by Matthew Syed, Wren & Rook 2018

**Your Mind Matters: Self-Esteem
and Confidence**
by Honor Head, Franklin Watts, 2017

GLOSSARY

anxiety a feeling of being worried and nervous

assertive being able to express your own opinions and wants in a way that is not aggressive

confident believing that you can do something

filtering removing something that is not wanted

inferior not as good

negative bad; negative feelings make you feel sad and miserable and not good enough

passive letting things happen even if you don't want them to

positive good; positive feelings make you feel strong and confident

posture the way you hold your body when you move

resentful angry or bitter

self-image how you see yourself

sluggish feeling slow and tired

visualise to see yourself doing something you want to achieve in your mind

INDEX